INSIGHT

KU-419-049

HONG KONG

Compact Guide: Hong Kong is the ideal quick-reference guide to this amazing metropolis. It tells you all you need to know about the city's attractions, from the temples of the gods to the temples of high finance, from simple markets to sophisticated superstores, as well as wonderful cuisine and fascinating festivals.

This is one of 130 Compact Guides, combining the interests and enthusiasms of two of the world's best-known information providers: Insight Guides, whose innovative titles have set the standard for visual travel guides since 1970, and Discovery Channel, the world's premier source of non-fiction television programming.

Discovery CHANNEL

APA PUBLICATIONS

Part of the Langenscheidt Publishing Group

Insight Compact Guide: Hong Kong

Written by: Franz-Josef Krücher
Updated by: Julie Gaw
Photography by: Bill Wassman
Additional photography by: courtesy of HKTB
Cover picture by: Chris Cormack/Impact Photos
Design: Vicky Pacey
Picture Editor: Hilary Genin
Cartographic Editor: Maria Randell
Maps: Dave Priestley

Editorial Director: Brian Bell
Managing Editor: Francis Dorai

CONTACTING THE EDITORS: As every effort is made to provide accurate information in this publication, we would appreciate it if readers would call our attention to any errors and omissions by contacting:
Apa Publications, PO Box 7910, London SE1 1WE, England.
Fax: (44 20) 7403 0290
e-mail: insight@apaguide.demon.co.uk

Information has been obtained from sources believed to be reliable, but its accuracy and completeness, and the opinions based thereon, are not guaranteed.

© 2003 APA Publications GmbH & Co. Verlag KG Singapore Branch, Singapore.

First Edition 1995
Third Edition 2003
Printed in Singapore by Insight Print Services (Pte) Ltd
Original edition © Polyglott-Verlag Dr Bolte KG, Munich

Worldwide distribution enquiries:
APA Publications GmbH & Co. Verlag KG (Singapore Branch)
38 Joo Koon Road, Singapore 628990
Tel: (65) 6865-1600, Fax: (65) 6861-6438

Distributed in the UK & Ireland by:
GeoCenter International Ltd
The Viables Centre, Harrow Way, Basingstoke,
Hampshire RG22 4BJ
Tel: (44 1256) 817 987, Fax: (44 1256) 817 988

Distributed in the United States by:
Langenscheidt Publishers, Inc.
46–35 54th Road, Maspeth, NY 11378
Tel: (1 718) 784 0055, Fax: (1 718) 784 0640

www.insightguides.com

HONG KONG

Introduction

Places

Culture

Travel Tips

△ **Sam Tung Uk Museum (p77)** This small walled village gives an insight into Hakka traditional life.

▽ **Bun Festival (p90)** Come each May, Pak Tai Temple in Cheung Chau Island is turned into a hive of activity by visitors celebrating the Bun Festival.

△ **Bank of China (p36)** The soaring tower on the right in Central is said to attract bad *fung shui* because of its sharp edges.

▷ **Ocean Park (p53)** Ride the cable car for the best views over this sprawling ocean-inspired theme park.

△ **Bronze Buddha (p87)** Keeping a watchful eye from its lofty position is this mammoth Buddha image in Lantau Island.

▷ **St John's (p37)** Purported to be the oldest Anglican cathedral in East Asia, this dates to 1849.

△ **Peak Tram (p49)**
Enjoy breathtaking views of the skyline as the Peak Tram chugs up the steep incline to Victoria Peak.

▷ **Temple Street (p65)**
When darkness falls, this street turns into a thriving open-air night market.

△ **Man Mo Temple (p25)** Look out for delicate swirls of incense hanging from the ceiling when visiting Chinese temples.

▽ **Star Ferry (p32)**
Don't miss the picturesque ride on board the Star Ferry, for only HK$2.20 a ticket.

Hong Kong – Fragrant Harbour

Crossing Hong Kong harbour on the Star Ferry, it seems hard to believe that the city's name is derived from the Cantonese phrase for 'Fragrant Harbour' – *Heung Gong*. But the evocative name probably derives from the trade in locally-grown incense wood, which once thrived at what is now Aberdeen. Another theory ascribes the name to the bauhinia, an aromatic flower which is native to the region.

The terminology is, in any case, confused, as the name 'Fragrant Harbour' sometimes refers to the entire territory, and sometimes only to the island of Hong Kong, the original colony lying off the Kowloon Peninsula.

The latter is also an anglicised version of the Chinese words for 'Nine Dragons'. These popular mythological creatures are the benevolent inhabitants of every mountain and the symbol of imperialism. A legend tells of the last emperor of the Song Dynasty (960–1279), who arrived on the peninsula after being ousted from his throne. When he remarked that he could see eight dragons – the mountains which later marked the frontier with the People's Republic of China – a court lackey remarked obsequiously that he must mean nine dragons, since he, the emperor, was also one.

Bauhinia
The Hong Kong Special Administrative Region's logo is a stylised five-petal bauhinia flower, with a star on each petal.

Opposite: a junk in the Hong Kong harbour with Central district in background Below: Tin Hau temple decoration

A GATEWAY TO CHINA

Hong Kong and China have always been inseparable. When the British flag was planted on what Lord Palmerston called the 'barren island' of Hong Kong in 1841, the colony quickly became an important trading post and gateway to China. Kowloon Peninsula and Stonecutters' Island were ceded in perpetuity in 1860 and the New Territories leased to the British for 99 years in 1898. All territories subsequently reverted to Chinese sovereignty in July 1997.

During the years of colonial rule, the efforts of the local, predominantly Chinese, population combined with the laissez-faire administration of the British to allow entrepreneurs to flourish here

as nowhere else on earth. As a result, Hong Kong has become a great international trading post, as well as a powerful manufacturing centre and a huge financial player.

Communist China could have repossessed Hong Kong at any time since 1949, but preferred instead to use it as a window on the Western world. Hong Kong's economy flourished as an effective export outlet for Chinese goods, which are now often manufactured under Hong Kong management on the mainland. Without the flow of Hong Kong capital and expertise, Chinese economic reforms would probably not have been able to get underway.

Government House

LOCATION AND SIZE

Situated between latitude 22°9' and 22°37' North and longitude 113°62' and 114°30' East, Hong Kong lies just inside the Tropic of Cancer on the same latitude as Calcutta and Havana. The total land area of 440 sq miles (1,098 sq km) – divided into the four main areas of Hong Kong Island, Kowloon, New Territories and the Outlying Islands – is constantly being altered by land reclamation projects.

Hong Kong lies off the northern delta of the Pearl River, through which traders could reach the provincial capital of Canton (present-day Guangzhou), the southern gateway to China. During the mid-19th century, the British were attracted primarily by the location of Hong Kong Island which forms a natural protective shield for the deep-water harbour.

Apart from the flat and sandy peninsula of Kowloon, Hong Kong is steeply mountainous; only 14 percent of the land mass is suitable for building. At 1,810ft (552m), Victoria Peak dominates Hong Kong Island, although Lantau Island has two considerably higher mountains: Lantau Peak, 3,064ft (934m) and Sunset Peak, 2,850ft (869m). The highest barrier in the chain of mountains in the New Territories is Tai Mo Shan at 3,136ft (956m).

CLIMATE

Hong Kong has a subtropical climate, characterised by high temperatures and high humidity. Late September to the end of December is the driest, most pleasant time to visit. The mercury drops in January and February to perhaps 10°C (50°F). March to mid-May brings wet, overcast weather, heralding the start of the hot, damp summer from late May to early September, with temperatures from 28° to 33°C (82° to 92°F). Year-round, clothing should be light and made of natural fibres.

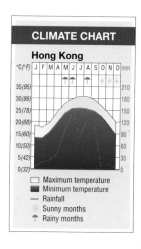

CLIMATE CHART

Hong Kong

☐ Maximum temperature
■ Minimum temperature
— Rainfall
☀ Sunny months
☂ Rainy months

LANDSCAPE AND ENVIRONMENT

Apart from the four main areas, Hong Kong Island, Kowloon, the New Territories and the Outlying Islands (including Lantau, Lamma and Cheung Chau), most of the 235 islands that make up Hong Kong are uninhabited. Like the open countryside of the larger islands and the New Territories, they are covered by evergreen undergrowth but few trees.

The visitor who expects to see a concrete jungle of skyscrapers will be surprised at how green the landscape actually is. There are 23 country parks which cover nearly 40 percent of the surface area. The visitor will have to search hard, however, to find the idyllic rice fields portrayed in old picture books. For decades, it has been

The Hong Kong Convention and Exhibition Centre

Below: Tai Lam Chung reservoir
Bottom: Hong Kong Park aviary

cheaper to import food from China than to grow it in Hong Kong. And the population of the New Territories has been on the upswing for years.

FLORA AND FAUNA

The flora of the region is subtropical, characterised by bamboo groves, palm trees and the odd rubber tree. Even within the city limits the occasional banyan tree, easily recognised by its remarkable overground root system, creeping over walls, has survived. Favourite decorative plants include bougainvillaea, hibiscus and orchid. Hong Kong's emblematic flower, the bauhinia (*Bauhinia blakeana*), or orchid tree, blooms a brilliant magenta from early November to March, while other species bloom white, yellow and pink throughout the rest of the year.

The diversity of habitat in Hong Kong encourages richness among local fauna, especially among birds and insects. More than 450 species of birds, 200 species of butterflies and 100 species of dragonflies have been recorded in the territory. Large birds of prey, called black-eared kites, are commonly seen circling above Hong Kong Island. Terrestrial mammals such as barking deer, macaques, wild pigs, leopard cats and porcupines inhabit rural areas of the New Territories but are scarcely seen.

Environmental Degradation

For all this abundance of nature, the development of Hong Kong has taken little account of the natural environment: sewage and industrial waste is often pumped directly into the sea; the air is often thick with the unfiltered fumes of factories, power stations and cars; and landscapes and marine fauna are destroyed as mountains are levelled to provide material for land reclamation.

This is not to say that there is no environmental protection in Hong Kong. The Mai Po marshes are an important conservation area. A sanctuary for migrating birds, Mai Po is also a favourite destination for bird-watchers; more than 360 species of birds have been recorded here. Lying partly in the no-man's land between Hong Kong and China, Mai Po's future is guaranteed by an international treaty.

> **Mai Po bird-watching**
> To visit the Mai Po Marshes, join the Mai Po Wetland Experience Tour with First Step Tours (www.firststep.com.hk; tel: 2366 5266; HK$350 per person), or contact the Hong Kong Tourism Board (tel: 2508 1234).

Hong Kong's People

Archaeological finds on the island of Lantau and at other sites prove that the region had been inhabited, albeit very thinly, for more than 6,000 years. When the British arrived in 1841, there were a number of little fishing villages along the coast and on the larger islands. They were primarily the home of the Tanka, who call themselves 'Water People' because they live on their boats. The literal translation, however, means 'Egg People', which may be due to the fact that they are purported to have paid taxes in eggs. The origins of the Tanka can be traced to the Malay Peninsula, which they left during the 8th century.

Another group of fishermen, the Hoklo, arrived during the 18th century from what is now the province of Fujian, settling in present-day Hong Kong and further, in Hainan island and across Southeast Asia.

Hakka and the Clans

By the time they were leased to Hong Kong in 1898, the New Territories were more densely and evenly populated. There were no towns as such,

Shopping at Pottinger Street

Talk of the town
In the street one hears virtually nothing but Cantonese spoken, though most taxi drivers and policemen speak at least a little English. In Hong Kong's hotels and restaurants, however, English is widely spoken, and all official signs and documents are bilingual.

but countless villages inhabited by peasants who worked the surrounding fields. Forty percent of the total of some 100,000 settlers were Hakka, whose ancestral home lay in the north of China but who had migrated ever further south, arriving here during the first half of the 18th century.

Women enjoy a privileged position in Hakka society, although they also work very hard physically. They are recognised by their broad-rimmed hats with black veils, and can be seen today working on the remaining fields as well as on the building sites in the city centre.

From the 10th century onwards, before the arrival of the Hakka, a wave of migration from other regions of China had gathered momentum.

The 'Five Great Clans' – the Tang, the Hau, the Pang, the Liu and the Man – were extended families who settled on the best agricultural land available and encouraged increasing numbers of relatives to join them. The Big Five clans now number many thousands, and can trace their family trees back by some 20 or 30 generations.

A Star Ferry sails in front of Central

RAPID URBANISATION

Hong Kong's present-day population of nearly 6.8 million is unevenly spread out. Mong Kok and the new town development of Kwun Tong (home to 50,100 people per sq km) are two of the world's most densely populated urban areas.

Following a fire in a shanty housing estate in 1953 which destroyed the homes of 60,000 people – most of them refugees from Communist China – the government drew up an ambitious social housing scheme which now sees half the population living in publicly subsidised housing.

Over the years, shopping complexes, sports halls, schools, cinemas, transport facilities and other amenities have been added to the infrastructure. From the beginning of the 1980s, vast housing estates called the New Towns were built in the New Territories.

Today, about half of the territory's population live in the New Territories, with 30 percent in Kowloon, and 20 percent on Hong Kong Island.

POPULATION

Approximately 95 percent of Hong Kong's citizens are Chinese. Foreigners form a tiny minority in comparison; even during the early colonial days they never made up more than 10 percent of the population. The Filipinos represent the largest foreign contingent, with some 142,500 nationals having settled in Hong Kong. The Indian minority, at 18,500, plays an important role in the local economy. Many Indian trading families arrived in Hong Kong during the 19th century in the wake of British colonial trade.

The make-up of the foreign population has changed with the Asian economic crisis: job losses led to a 25 percent drop in the Japanese population (14,175 in 2001), and a near doubling in the number of Indonesians, making them the second largest foreign group at 50,500.

Below: members of Hong Kong's Sikh community
Bottom: New Territories housing by night

LANGUAGE

The official languages in Hong Kong are English and Cantonese. Although English is taught in every school, only a small percentage of the population speak it fluently. Local residents are more eager to learn Putonghua, or Mandarin Chinese, which is used in mainland China. The two languages share the same written characters, although the mainland uses a simplified version.

GOVERNMENT AND ECONOMY

Hong Kong reverted to China on 1 July 1997. Under an arrangement referred to as 'One Country, Two Systems', Hong Kong is now a Special Administrative Region (HKSAR) of China, and promised a high degree of autonomy. The Sino-British Joint Declaration on the future of Hong Kong, signed in 1984, stated that Hong Kong's capitalist lifestyle shall remain unchanged for 50 years after 1997; it will be free to continue its own political, social and economic systems; and will enjoy a high degree of autonomy except in foreign and defence affairs. These and other assurances were enshrined in the Basic Law, promulgated by China in 1990.

Below: a symbol of Chinese rule
Bottom: Wanchai street market

Hong Kong is governed by the HKSAR Executive Council, the main policy-making body whose chief executive is Mr Tung Chee-Hwa – now in his second term – and the HKSAR Legislative Assembly, which is responsible for framing legislation, enacting the laws and controlling the budget. The territory's judicial independence and the rule of law were assured by the Basic Law.

However, Hong Kong's autonomy was seriously undermined in June 1999 when the National People's Congress in Beijing overturned a ruling by the territory's highest court, the Court of Final Appeal, which would have granted abode to an estimated 1.67 million mainlanders.

TRADING POST BEGINNINGS

Before the Asian economic crisis that began in 1997, Hong Kong was dubbed one of the 'Four Little Tigers' of Asia which demonstrated enormous economic growth and rapid industrialisation in the wake of Japan's industrial expansion after World War II.

Hong Kong's beginnings were modest enough: founded as a trading post, the colony produced virtually no income, as it was a free port from the start. Leasing and auctioning the small area of land available brought the government less money than it spent on infrastructure and defence.

Following the communist takeover in China in 1949, many who had cause to fear the new rulers fled the country to Hong Kong. Among them were businessmen, especially from Shanghai, which had been China's boom city during the 1920s.

They invested the capital they brought with them in Hong Kong and followed Japan's example in accelerating the industrialisation process by means of simple products in the textile and plastics industries. In small factories, workers toiled virtually round the clock under unspeakably poor conditions for very low wages. Their appetite for survival created the East Asian economic miracle.

MANUFACTURING BOOM

Having no raw materials which were worth very much, except the most valuable raw material of all – energetic people hungry for success, Hong Kong developed into a manufacturing city which, bearing in mind its small local population, was obliged to export 90 percent of its goods. The second act of the 'miracle' saw a larger range of products and a greater attention to quality.

By the late 1970s, the territory was diversifying into new product development – everything from electronics to the latest fashions. Economic and population growth increased Hong Kong's dependence on imports.

The territory could not survive without food, water and energy from the mainland. After

Early trade
Hong Kong's early industries were associated with the port: shipbuilding and repairs, fishing and the supply of provisions for migrants. Trade assumed pride of place and, for a long time, the scene was dominated by the two commodities which had precipitated the British annexation of Hong Kong: tea and opium.

Central by night

Chinese leader Deng Xiaoping's economic reforms in 1978, the interconnection between Hong Kong and its powerful neighbour became even closer, with Hong Kong handling a considerable proportion of Chinese exports through its trading, financial and transport infrastructure.

Close Ties with China

Hong Kong's investment of vast amounts of money, staff and expertise in mainland China was reciprocated by the establishment of mainland companies in the territory and the mainland purchase of shares in Hong Kong enterprises.

Hong Kong thus evolved into a service economy. Work-intensive manufacturing industries were transferred to China's Special Economic Zones, set up in the early 1980s to stimulate rapid economic growth in strategic coastal areas, without rocking socialism in the rest of China, and in other regions with low wages.

Tourist arrivals

Despite the worldwide downturn in the travel and tourism industry following 9/11, visitor arrivals to Hong Kong have actually been increasing. Although foreign arrivals are down, an increasing number of mainland Chinese tourists have been coming to town – a situation that seems likely to continue, and bodes well for the city.

Visitors to the Hong Kong Cultural Centre

Economic Miracle

Although still suffering from the economic downturn that started in October 1997, Hong Kong remains a major international trading and financial centre. It is the second largest stock market in Asia after Tokyo (and the 10th largest in the world), the 10th largest banking centre, and the seventh largest foreign exchange market in the world. It is also a major transport hub; home to the world's busiest container port (with a throughput of 17.9 million TEUs annually) and one of its busiest international air cargo terminals.

Support for the pure market economy is still virtually unanimous. The laws governing social services are minimal. Social insurance and sickness insurance have only been part of the scene for the past few years. Tax laws are very straightforward and provide the government with so much money that its reserves are growing steadily. Income and business taxes hover between 15 and 17 percent; capital gains are not taxed at all.

PRESENT-DAY RECESSION

But deflationary forces unleashed by the economic crisis are still at work. By July 2002 unemployment figures had risen to 7.7 percent and consumer price index dropped to 3.4 percent.

The budget deficit has also become a concern due to poor land sales, from which the government traditionally derives the bulk of its income. Proposals to introduce a 1 percent sales tax, calls by the local sector to reduce foreign maids' salaries and a continued rise in personal and company bankruptcies in 2002 reflect the current economic climate. Even before the recession, long working hours, minimal holidays, poor working conditions and a polluted environment were downsides to Hong Kong's economic success story.

It remains to be seen how Hong Kong will weather the recession and the threat to its judicial autonomy. But, as China's main economic window on the world, it remains in the mainland's self-interest for Hong Kong to survive and flourish as a dynamic and unfettered financial and service hub. The chances of an economic recovery for Hong Kong are looking good following China's entry into the World Trade Organization (WTO), as the granting of WTO status should benefit the thousands of Hong Kong companies that conduct a global business via the mainland.

Below: a Kowloon shop
Bottom: public telephones in the New Territories

HISTORICAL HIGHLIGHTS

c 4,000BC Archaeological finds on Lamma and Lantau islands indicate Stone Age settlement of the coastal strip.

c 1,200BC Tools and pots dating from the Bronze Age found. Engravings on rock surfaces also date from this era.

7th–9th centuries AD Probable arrival of Tanka people. Chinese fortress constructed in Tuen Mun.

10th–14th centuries Arrival of the 'Five Great Clans' in what is now the New Territories.

Early 16th century Portuguese traders are the first Europeans to reach Canton. Imperial troops expel Portuguese from Tuen Mun.

1557 Portugal establishes official trading colony at Macau.

1714 Canton opened to foreign trade; British East India Company (EIC) establishes itself.

1773 The EIC unloads 150 pounds of Bengal opium at Canton.

1799 Peking bans the opium drug trade, but smuggling by British traders is rife.

Early 19th century The EIC trading monopoly collapses. The opium trade is taken over by independent British and American traders. The British government hopes to open several Chinese ports to overseas trade.

1839 For economic reasons the Chinese imperial court again bans the trade in opium, commandeering and burning the stocks in Canton. The British retaliate by shooting at Chinese guard posts, sparking the First Opium War.

1841 A British fleet under Captain Charles Elliot attacks Canton and takes possession of Hong Kong by hoisting the Union Jack at Possession Point on 26 January.

1842 China cedes Hong Kong Island to the British 'in perpetuity' in the 'unequal' Treaty of Nanking. Sir Henry Pottinger becomes the first governor.

1856–60 Dissatisfied with the opportunities for trade with China, the British embark on the Second Opium War and force the opening of further ports and the cession of the Kowloon Peninsula in the Convention of Peking.

1898 Britain negotiates a 99-year lease of the New Territories and the 233 Outlying Islands, until 30 June 1997. The Star Ferry commences operation.

1910 The Kowloon–Canton Railway to the China border is completed.

1911 Qing dynasty falls; Sun Yat-sen forms the Republic of China.

1928 Mao Zedong establishes his first guerrilla base; by 1935 he has taken control of the Chinese Communist Party.

1937–45 Japanese troops attack China via Korea and precipitate a growing tide of refugees in Hong Kong. Shortly after the bombing of Pearl Harbour in 1941, the Japanese air force destroys British aircraft at Hong Kong's Kai Tak airport. The army advances through the New Territories and forces the defending troops to retreat to Hong Kong Island, where they surrender during Christmas 1941. The Japanese army sets up concentration camps, deports workers and forces thousands to flee. Hong Kong loses one million inhabitants.

1945 The Yalta Conference rules that Hong Kong should be returned to the victorious Chinese; however, the civil war which raged on the mainland until 1949 prevented this decision from being put into practice. A British military administration builds up the colony again and hands it over to a new British governor.

1950 UN embargo on trade with China and North Korea during the Korean War seriously depresses the entrepôt trade, the lifeline of the colony – conditions remain depressed for several years.

1950–3 The communist victory on mainland China sees massive waves of refugees swell the local population. Industrialisation commences.

Early 1960s Poor pay and working conditions in factories lead to labour disputes and increasing social discontent.

1966–9 The Cultural Revolution in China spreads to Hong Kong via communist cell strikes by workers and taxi drivers. In May 1967, severe riots break out following a labour dispute in a plastic-flower factory. Beijing intervenes to prevent the planned general strike, thus ensuring that Hong Kong remains China's secret trade outlet.

1970 The first jumbo jet touches down at Kai Tak Airport.

1972 Richard Nixon visits China. The Cross Harbour Tunnel opens.

1978 The death of Mao Zedong (1976) is followed by power struggles from which the economic reformers emerge victorious. Hong Kong's economic interconnection with China grows apace, especially following the establishment of the Special Economic Zone of Shenzen on the border. China campaigns for the return of the colony.

1984 Margaret Thatcher and Chinese premier Zhao Ziyang sign the Joint Declaration for the return of the entire Hong Kong territory to China on 1 July 1997.

1989 Hong Kong residents take to the streets in shocked protests at the 4 June 'pro-democracy crackdown' in Tiananmen Square, Beijing.

1990 China promulgates the Basic Law as a blueprint for Hong Kong's constitution after 1997, endorsing the aims and assurances of the Joint Declaration.

1992 Chris Patten takes over as the last British governor.

1993–6 The Sino-British relationship deteriorates as the Chinese government spurns attempts by the British administration to introduce last-minute democratic reforms to the colony. Discussions about the practical transfer of power continue behind closed doors.

1997 China resumes sovereignty. Tung Chee-Hwa, a shipping magnate, is appointed the first Chief Executive, leading a Beijing-appointed Provisional Legislature. The Hong Kong Stock Market dives on the back of the region-wide Asian economic crisis.

1998 First HKSAR Legco elections. The Hong Kong International Airport at Chek Lap Kok opens. The economy continues its downward spiral.

1999 The Basic Law is undermined as the government asks Beijing to overturn the Court of Final Appeal's ruling on the 'right of abode'.

2002 Tung Chee-Hwa runs unopposed and is appointed by Beijing for a second term as Chief Executive. Unemployment reaches an all-time high of 7.7 percent in July.

Map on pages 24–25

1: Western District

Central–Mid-Levels Escalator – SoHo – Hollywood Road – Man Mo Temple – Museum of Medical Sciences – Cat Street – Queen's Road West – Bonham Strand West – Western Market – Man Wa Lane chop carvers

Beneath all the skyscrapers and other temples to business and commerce still thrives a traditional way of life. There is no better way for visitors to immerse themselves in the city's everyday street life than by heading westward on Hong Kong Island to explore the antique shops, the old temples, the flea market, the chemists, the paper shops, the rice merchants and the pawnbrokers.

Wander through the market for dried foodstuffs, and take home a Chinese seal (or 'chop') with your name carved on it as a reminder of this three-hour stroll through traditional Hong Kong. This tour is best taken around mid-morning or early afternoon to catch the street markets and shops in full swing.

City info

Before setting off on your trek through the Western district, stop by the Hong Kong Tourism Board (HKTB) Visitor Information Centre (daily 8am–6pm) on the ground floor of The Center, where you'll find plenty of handy pamphlets, maps and events information, all free of charge.

Preceding pages: Hong Kong's glittering skyline Below: the steel-and-glass facade of The Center

MID-LEVELS

Opposite the headquarters of the Hang Seng Bank, **Central Market ❶** stands as one of the largest wet markets in Hong Kong. To stroll around the

ground floor meat stalls or teeming second-storey vegetable stands, be sure to arrive before noon, when activities wind down for the day and the vendors head off to lunch. Across Jubilee Street stands the gleaming 80-storey tower of **The Center**, an imposing 1,149-ft (350-m) office complex completed in 1998.

From Central Market, the 2,500-ft (800-m) ★ **Central–Mid-Levels Escalator** ❷, the world's longest covered outdoor escalator system, runs up to the prime residential district of **Mid-Levels** as far as Conduit Road. Designed to relieve traffic congestion in the narrow city streets, the escalator whisks financiers, traders and housewives on shopping sprees downhill every morning to **Central**, the financial district. Come 10.20am, the escalator is switched to an uphill direction until midnight, affording glimpses of apartment windows en route and, from the top, a bird's-eye view of the mêlée of cars and people in the alleys below.

A sharp right-hand bend with an old colonial-style police station on the left marks the start of Hollywood Road. The ★ **Central Police Station Compound** ❸ (1864–1925) is one of the finest examples of early colonial architecture left. Though it's not officially open to the public, you may be allowed to look round if you report in first. **Victoria Prison**, behind, was built in 1841 and is still in use, holding illegal immigrants – predominantly overstayers from the mainland.

SOHO

Anyone feeling peckish may continue up the escalator to ★ **SoHo** ❹, where a wide range of cuisines are available in a remarkably compact area. **Staunton Street** and **Elgin Street**, just off the escalator, form the heart of SoHo (meaning South of Hollywood Road). The nouveau dining area sprung up in 1995, much to the chagrin of local residents who preferred the relative peace and quiet of their traditional noodle shops, market stalls, chemists and artisans' shops.

Nevertheless, the Chinese have proven to be rather adaptable: today the mom-and-pop corner

Below: Central–Mid-Levels Escalator
Bottom: Central Police Station

Map below

Lan Kwai Fong by night

stores sell sundries like cat food and toilet paper alongside fine wines. When it comes to food, choose from Nepalese (**Sherpa**), Italian (**Al Dente** or **Sole Mio**), Spanish (**La Comida**), fusion (**Jaspa's**), Cuban (**Cubana**), Thai (**Tom Yums**), Mexican (**Caramba**), French (**2 Sardines**) or Russian (**Troika**). SoHo swarms with revellers come happy hour, though it's more for sustenance than for late-night drinking. After dinner, make like the local expats and roll down the hill to the fashionable watering holes of **Lan Kwai Fong** *(see also pages 112–3)* tucked just below Hollywood Road.

HOLLYWOOD ROAD

In sharp contrast to the international flavours of SoHo, Chinese culture comes firmly into focus through the **Hollywood Road** shop windows, filled with antiques galore. There are tiny snuff bottles painted on the inside, every imaginable item of porcelain: dishes, plates, bowls, vases,

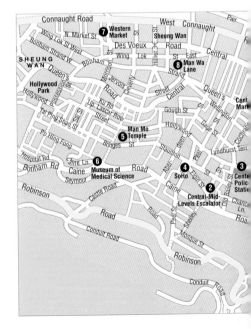

statues and other decorative figures, furniture, miniature embroidered shoes for bound feet, Tibetan chests still redolent of yak butter, and, of course, temple statues from the tiny God of Literature to bronze Buddhas.

Buyers should be aware that not all items on display are genuine, and prices are often exorbitantly high. The market is being flooded not only with the booty of grave robbers, but also with cheap imitations from China. Certificates of authenticity are regularly falsified and even experts are sometimes fooled.

MAN MO TEMPLE

Hollywood Road used to be lined with three- and four-storey houses, but these are gradually being demolished to make way for new high-rise blocks. The ★★ **Man Mo Temple** ❺ is a remnant of old Hong Kong. It was built in around 1842 by the notorious pirate Cheung Po-tsai after he abandoned his old way of life and entered government

Shopping tips
The Hollywood Road antique shops closer to the escalator tend to sell wooden furniture and small collectibles, such as Chinese cabinets, altar tables, elaborately carved screens and wildly expensive trays made of precious *zitan* wood. Heading west, the shops thin out a bit and sell more statuary and ceramics. (The words 'tomb raider' may come to mind.) Prices are rather excessive along this entire strip of prime real estate, but it never hurts to look. Bargain hunters will be better served scouring shops in southern China or nearby Macau, or even the warehouse shops of Ap Lei Chau (see Shopping, page 116).

Hollywood Road antique displays

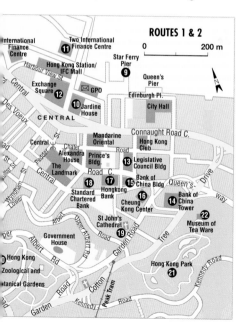

ROUTES 1 & 2

0   200 m

International Finance Centre ⓫ Two International Finance Centre
Star Ferry Pier ❾
Hong Kong Station/ IFC Mall
Harbour View St
Queen's Pier
Exchange Square ⓬ ✉ GPO
Edinburgh Pl.
Des Voeux
⓾ Jardine House
City Hall
CENTRAL
Connaught Road C.
Central
Chater Alexandra House
Mandarine Oriental
Hong Kong Club
Prince's Bldg. ⓭ Legislative Council Bldg
Pedder
The Landmark
Road C
Bank of China Bldg ⓯
Queen's Drive
Standard Chartered Bank ⓲
Hongkong Bank ⓯
Cheung Kong Center ⓰
Bank of China Tower ⓮
Wyndham
Lower
St John's Cathedral
Upper Albert Rd
Museum of Tea Ware ㉒
Government House
⓳
Garden Road
Tree
Albert Rd
Hong Kong Park ㉑
Hong Kong Zoological and Botanical Gardens
Cotton
Peak Tram
Kennedy Road
Garden
Kennedy Road

Map
on pages
24–25

Incense coils grace the ceiling of Man Mo Temple

service. The temple is dedicated to Man, the God of Literature, who is revered by academics and officials, and Mo, the God of War, who attracts large numbers of policemen, pawnbrokers and antique dealers. Statues of the 10 kings of heaven guard the entrance.

On the side wall are litters in which the statues are borne through the streets during the temple festival. Man wears a green garment and carries a calligrapher's brush. Mo wears a red garment and holds an executioner's sword. The altar on the left is dedicated to the black-faced god of justice, Bao Gong, and the one on the right to the city deity, Shing Wong. The air inside the temple is usually heavy with incense.

LADDER STREET

Outside on Hollywood Road, **Ladder Street** to the left, literally climbs up the hill. The name 'street' is actually an exaggeration, but 'ladder' is appropriate enough. Today, the steps are concreted, but it is not hard to imagine two skinny coolies toiling up under the burden of a portly European in a sedan chair in times of yore.

Ladder Street leads up to the ★ **Museum of Medical Sciences** ❻ (Tuesday to Saturday 10am–5pm; Sunday and some public holidays 1pm–5pm; admission fee) – a fascinating collection of traditional Chinese and modern Western medicine housed in the old Pathological Institute (1906) on Caine Lane.

Coming back to Hollywood Road, Ladder Street leads on to what the locals call ★★ **Cat Street**, although its official name is Upper Lascar Row. The nickname may refer to the cat burglars who sold their stolen goods here. Some also say that the street gained its name because the Chinese equivalent of a flea market is a 'mouse market' and the purchasers, therefore, are the 'cats'.

Upper Lascar Row was once the heart of a crowded ghetto, and antiques and second-hand goods have been traded here for 150 years. During the afternoon, elderly men spread out mats and rugs on the ground in order to display their wares: amulets, jade, watches and other bric-a-brac. Some traders have proper stalls with a wider range of goods, and the street is also lined with antique and furniture shops.

POSSESSION STREET

Back on Hollywood Road, continue eastwards until you reach **Possession Street**, on the right. It is hard to imagine now, but this used to be the waterfront, and Possession Street marks the spot where a decisive chapter of Hong Kong's history was written. Captain Charles Elliot landed in January 1841 and took possession of the island here in the name of the British crown – somewhat hastily, as it turned out, because Her Majesty's Government would have preferred an island off the coast of Shanghai.

Anyway, more than a year was to pass before the island was finally ceded following a few threatening gestures by the British warships off Nanking, which was the Chinese capital at the time. Elliot was summoned back to England because of his excessive zeal, instead of becoming the first governor. That honour was reserved for Sir Henry Pottinger.

A few yards further on is **Hollywood Road Park**, a modern interpretation of the traditional Chinese city garden. Old sepia photos on the

Star Attraction
● Cat Street

Stepping up
Even the squeamish can appreciate the Hong Kong Museum of Medical Sciences *(see opposite)*, housed in a lovely British colonial building of Edwardian design, and echoed in the YMCA building, which you'll pass on the long walk up. Museum standouts include a radiology exhibit featuring X-rays of a woman with bound feet, a wood-panelled basement room decorated as an herbalists' shop, an old dentist's chair and a 1950s green vinyl operating table. To get there, just follow the signs up Ladder Street and be sure to pace yourself. The walk should take no more than 5 minutes.

Cat Street vendor

Map
on pages
24–25

notice board show how the area looked a century ago. This welcome green space is a meeting place for local residents, where birds sing from cages, wizened old men gather for card games, grey-haired ladies perform graceful *tai chi* exercises and children chase after plastic footballs.

TO THE AFTERLIFE

The route soon arrives at **Queen's Road West**, another shopping street where household goods are offered alongside Chinese foodstuffs, especially a variety of rice in huge burlap sacks. The visitor will be struck by the paper models of houses, cars, motorcycles, furniture, etc. Fake paper money with an astronomically high face value, made out by the 'Bank of the Underworld', is stacked high in the shops.

The items in question are not toys but gifts to be ceremonially burned on the graves of the deceased so that the dead can enjoy the 'good life' in the 'great beyond'.

Come January, the shops are usually flush with red objects – calendars, banners, gift boxes and small bags – as the colour is considered to be lucky. At Chinese New Year, families redecorate their homes and distribute presents. The most popular presents are *lai see*, little red envelopes containing 'lucky' money.

Chinese take-away

The locals go to great lengths to keep their ancestors happy in the afterlife. Beyond the paper models of houses and cars, one can purchase shoes and clothing (though no brand names just yet!), face cream and other cosmetics, karaoke machines and even air conditioners, all made of paper. Knowing the penchant that Hong Kongers have for eating out, there are also boxes of faux sushi, and entire trays of paper hamburgers, fries and a soda, mimicking McDonald's packaging. Better order that meal 'to go'.

Queen's Road West is a hive of activity

Turn right into Sutherland Street. At the end of the road and in the wider expanse of **Des Voeux Road West**, which can be distinguished by the tram lines which pass along it, there are countless shops offering dried foodstuffs, including mushrooms, scallops and shrimps, fruit, lotus nuts, sunflower seeds, pine kernels, biscuits and sweets.

The fried mushrooms taste especially good; they simply need to be soaked in boiling water for a few minutes to make them tender and tasty once more.

Below: Hollywood Road Park
Botttom: dried goods at
Bonham Strand West

BONHAM STRAND WEST

In this district, streets named after the various governors adjoin one another. Sir Samuel Bonham (1848–54) leads off directly from Sir William Des Voeux (1887–91). The former, also known as **Bonham Strand West**, is home to shops selling dried foods, many alien to Western cuisine but considered by the Chinese to be gourmet delicacies. Bonham Strand West is the headquarters of the firms which import abalone, sharks' fins, swallows' nests and ginseng. Ginseng is a root which grows primarily in Korea, in very finely sieved, humus-rich soil and which is dug up after several years. It is claimed that ginseng possesses healing as well as aphrodisiac properties; the latter is also claimed of abalone and sharks' fin.

Swallows' nests, cemented by the saliva of swallows, are harvested in Thailand and Vietnam by daring young men who retrieve the nests from cliffs when the young birds have hatched. In Bonham Strand West it is also possible to catch a glimpse inside the workshops where these foodstuffs are sorted, cut and packed.

WESTERN MARKET

Turning left, the route passes metalworkers' shops before arriving at a modern multi-storey market. Many stallholders here were previously housed in the colonial building of ★ **Western Market ❼** (daily 10am–7pm). The latter, a red-brick building with beige decorative brickwork, can be reached by following a narrow road on the left-

Map
on pages
24–25

hand side. Built in 1906, it is a fine example of Edwardian architecture. Fortunately, when it became too small and unhygienic after 83 years of service, the building was not torn down like most other buildings dating from this period, but was sensitively restored and re-opened in 1991 as a period shopping mall.

The fabric merchants upstairs relocated when the Cloth Alley bazaar on Wing On Street was demolished, and their prices are fair. Downstairs shops sell mostly tourist kitsch and Coca-Cola collectibles, but the red London telephone boxes at the end are certainly attractive.

Western Market's most attractive facade is on Connaught Road and is best viewed from the pedestrian overpass leading to the Macau Ferry Terminal. To sample a traditional dim sum lunch, you can visit the **Treasure Inn Seafood Restaurant** upstairs, which features an English menu with pictures of the dishes. Traditional dim sum favourites include *char shao bao* (barbecued pork buns), *ha gau* (shrimp dumplings) and *siu mai* (pork dumplings).

Below: dim sum selection
Bottom: a chop carver

SEALS OF APPROVAL

The entire district is full of quaint and practical shops to interest the visitor. To put the seal of approval on this encounter with Chinese everyday life, visit one of Hong Kong's famous **chop carvers**. These chops, or seals, with engraved characters are thought to have been in use in China for some 3,000 years. In former times, bronze, ivory, jade, amber, horn or crystallised stones were used for chops. Today, the most common materials are clay, porcelain, bamboo, soapstone or plastic, the best material being a reddish stone known as 'Chicken's Blood'.

MAN WA LANE

Most of the chop carvers are located on ★ **Man Wa Lane ❽**, a narrow alley running between Wing Lok Street (near the Sheung Wan MTR exit) and Bonham Strand (beside the HSBC branch).

After surveying the goods on offer, choose a stone, a script type, and the way in which your name should be written.

Latin script is not a problem; if Chinese characters are preferred, the carver will have to transcribe your name phonetically by means of appropriate symbols.

However, a true Chinese name also has a meaning which is closely linked to the character of its owner. Only a Chinese acquaintance who knows something about you will be able to give you such a name. In this case, ask the person to write it down for the chop carver.

MODERN SCRIPT

The oldest Chinese characters, traditionally used on seals, were introduced during the reign of the first king of the unifield kingdom (221–206BC), Emperor Qin Shi Huangdi. The various strokes are grouped into rectangles with rounded corners to form the so-called official script. Many chop carvers are no longer fluent in this script, and so the newer everyday characters are also used.

Chops generally take from one to four hours to make, although complicated commissions may take longer. It is usual to make a down payment. Some carvers can also produce business cards on small hand printing presses.

Chop-chop

Even today, in the quintessentially modern business environment of Hong Kong, a chop serves the same function as a signature. When courier companies drop packages off at an office, they turn their nose up at signatures and give their seal of approval only to the official company chop. In traditional China, chops would serve as signatures at the end of letters or contracts and also indicate ownership.

Thus, pictures were signed not only by the artist on completion, but also by the purchaser. Prosperous Chinese officials would often possess a variety of seals charting their personal progress and development. Scholars laid great store by attractive and valuable seals.

Chop carver at work in Man Wa Lane

Philately
Stamp collectors will be pleasantly thrilled with the array of stamps for sale at the Philatelic Centre on the ground floor of the General Post Office *(see opposite)*. There is also a Postal Gallery, showing quaint old British post boxes and delivery bikes still used in villages of the New Territories.

2: Central

Star Ferry – Jardine House – International Finance Centre – Exchange Square – Legco – Bank of China – Hongkong Bank – St John's Cathedral – Government House – Zoological and Botanical Gardens – Hong Kong Park

When the British settled in their new colony, they called the capital Victoria, after their queen, who nearly rejected the island to which her foreign secretary, Lord Palmerston, disparagingly referred as a 'barren island'.

Today, the built-up area extends right along the north coast – its heart the **Central** district, the financial and business hub. The headquarters of Hong Kong's principal banks mark the architectural highlights of Central. Here too are the shopping centres and *haute couture* boutiques. Yet, just a couple of hundred metres beyond the towering skyscrapers you can relax in the Zoological and Botanical Gardens or Hong Kong Park. Allow two to three hours for this tour.

STAR FERRY

Star Ferry with Hong Kong Island skyline in background

The route begins by the **Star Ferry Pier** ❾ from where the photogenic green and white ferries have been steaming across the harbour since 1898. A

Star Attraction
● Star Ferry ride

★★Star Ferry ride at night is a highlight of any stay in Hong Kong. Like the trams *(see page 41)*, this ride is a bargain, at HK$2.20. Directly adjacent lies the **Queen's Pier**, the government's official landing stage where private boats may also moor to take on passengers.

Opposite, **City Hall**, a utilitarian 1962 building, houses a library, marriage registry, various city administration offices and one of Hong Kong's major cultural entertainment venues. Events information and tickets are available in the lobby. The attractive inner courtyard is decorated with trees and sculptures, which makes it a popular place for newly-wed couples fresh from the Registry Office to pause for their first photos.

Leaving the City Hall, the oddly inverted highrise to the east, formerly the Prince of Wales Building, is now called the **Chinese People's Liberation Army Forces Hong Kong Building**. Its original tenants, the British armed forces, handed it over to the PLA in 1997.

JARDINE HOUSE

The city's last remaining rickshaw drivers usually assemble on the covered exit path from the Star Ferry. Most are delighted to pose for a photo – but strictly in exchange for dollars, so ask first before shooting. These two-wheeled conveyances first appeared in Hong Kong in the 1870s.

Around the corner is a site for philatelists, the **General Post Office**. It offers exhibitions of historic and commemorative stamps and a card shop, as well as the usual postal services.

The tower just across the road is the 50-storey **Jardine House ❿**, whose 1,748 round windows have inspired the Chinese to nickname it the 'House of a Thousand Orifices'. Jardine's is one of the oldest trading houses in the city; its colourful history provided much of the inspiration for James Clavell's famous novels about Hong Kong: *Tai Pan* and *Noble House*.

Directly across Connaught Road stands the newly-unveiled glass façade of the **Chater House**, a high-rent office building.

Below: posing outside City Hall
Bottom: Jardine House's signature windows

Map
on pages
24–25

> **Tai chi in bronze**
> If you visit Ju Ming's Tai Chi statue at Exchange Square early in the morning, you may see the real thing: this is a favourite spot for *tai chi* practice. Even the early-morning light hitting the statue itself is enough to energise you for the day.

INTERNATIONAL FINANCE CENTRE

The waterfront used to continue west of the Star Ferry, but has now moved further out into the harbour, as part of a massive land reclamation scheme to create more space for the Airport Express terminus, **Hong Kong Station** and the **International Finance Centre** development.

Included in the IFC complex are the One International Finance Centre, the massive IFC Mall and the 88-storey, harbourfront **Two International Finance Centre** ⓫. Slated to open in late 2003, Two IFC will supersede Central Plaza *(see page 44)* as the tallest building in Hong Kong, at 420 metres (1,378ft). Next door will stand the new Four Seasons Hotel and the exclusive Four Seasons Service Suites.

EXCHANGE SQUARE AREA

Behind the IFC, the tinted glass and pink granite **Exchange Square** ⓬ is home to the Hong Kong Stock Exchange (no visitors). Art galleries frequently use the lobby of the **Rotunda**, or upper lobby of One and Two Exchange Square, for exhibitions. The podium courtyard outside is decorated by fountains and bronze sculptures, ★ **Water Buffalo** by Dame Elizabeth Frink, a Henry Moore sculpture and a powerful statue called ★ **Tai Chi Player** by Ju Ming. **La Fontaine** café to the side of the Tai Chi statue is a good place for refreshments and people watching. A trendy watering hole, **In-X**, occupies the opposite side.

The windows above the curved entrance to the rather squat **Forum** building represent stylised Chinese coins, which were round with square holes in the middle, through which they were threaded with string for safe keeping.

The underpass south of the Star Ferry Concourse leads to the **Mandarin Oriental** one of the world's top hotels, and a social institution in Hong Kong. Its lobby lounge, restaurants and bars, including top-floor **Vong** (tel: 2825 4028), are popular rendezvous points for local residents.

At lunchtime, however, office workers are just as likely to be seen with a sandwich in hand at

Henry Moore sculpture at Exchange Square

Statue Square next door. On Sunday, the square and surrounding streets are chock-a-block with people, particularly Filipino domestic workers (or *amahs*) who gather here on their day off. In the north section of the square is a cenotaph commemorating the dead of two world wars.

LEGCO BUILDING

The **Hong Kong Club** can be recognised by its narrow windows. The most powerful men in the city meet here, and their decisions have always been more far reaching than those made in the nearby domed ★ **Legislative Council Building (Legco)** ⑬, Hong Kong's equivalent of a parliament. The neo-classical building previously housed the Supreme Court, the colony's final court of appeal. The foundation stone was laid in 1903, but construction was not completed until 1912.

Below: Legco Building
Bottom: lunchtime crowds at Statue Square

After the court moved to purpose-built law courts in Wanchai, the building underwent extensive interior alterations. In 1984, as the only colonial building remaining in the city centre, it was placed under a protection order. Sittings are held every Wednesday when Legco is in session (open to the public by prior reservation, tel: 2869 9399).

On the opposite side of the Hong Kong Club is the **Ritz-Carlton Hotel**, another prestigious address in town. Cigar aficionados head for **The**

Map
on pages
24–25

Below: Hong Kong bank Building
Bottom: Bank of China Tower is based on multiple triangles

Nurse cigar bar, while movers and shakers more traditionally head for **Toscana** (tel: 2877 6666), the Ritz's fine Italian dining restaurant featuring innovative Tuscan cuisine. Another popular restaurant is **Shanghai Shanghai** (tel: 2877 6666) in the basement, with the Art Deco feel of 1930s Shanghai – and with a live 'golden oldies' performance nightly on the bandstand (closed Sunday).

BANK OF CHINA

Across Queen's Road soars the Hong Kong headquarters of the ★★ **Bank of China Tower ⑭**. Its 1209-ft (369-m) tower is a landmark on the city skyline. The American-Chinese architect I.M. Pei demonstrated the power of Hong Kong's new rulers with this spectacular blue-glass skyscraper, supposedly inspired by the way that bamboo grows ever skyward, section upon section.

In 1982, the bank obtained the site from the Hong Kong government for a friendly HK$1.1 billion, but financing problems and construction delays meant the bank was not ready for use until May 1990. The building attracted criticism from *fung shui* experts for its exterior form and general structure based on multiple triangles. Some say the angles direct bad *chi* towards the Legco Building.

Its predecessor, the old **Bank of China Building ⑮**, opposite Legco, seems almost modest in

comparison. It is an attractive stone art deco-style building dating from 1950. The top floors, where the economic section of the Communist Party once met, today form an elegant rendezvous for Hong Kong's movers and shakers, who meet in the members-only **China Club** with its lavish Shanghai furnishings and an impressive collection of modern Chinese art.

Towering between the two is the boxy 62-storey **Cheung Kong Center** ⑯, headquarters for renowned property tycoon Li Kai-shing's Cheung Kong Group. Built by architects Leo Daly and Cesar Pelli, the reflective glass and stainless steel modern building is quite a sight.

MORE SWANKY BANKS

The imposing building next door is the nerve centre of the ★★ **Hongkong Bank (HSBC)** ⑰, known in the city by the understated abbreviation, 'The Bank'. Sir Norman Foster designed the building according to bridge-building principles and intentionally positioned technical facilities and services on the exterior, including those which are normally carefully hidden away. Completed in 1985 at a cost of US$1 billion, the building remains one of Hong Kong's most impressive landmarks. It is worth taking the escalators up to the banking halls in order to appreciate the scale of the 170-ft (52-m) atrium.

The narrow reddish tower on the right is the headquarters of the **Standard Chartered Bank** ⑱. From the 21st storey upwards, the floor area is reduced every six floors. In contrast to its major competitor, the building's design is based on the octagon, which delighted the geomancers.

A COLONIAL FLAIR

Passing beneath Hongkong Bank, cross Queen's Road and climb the steps leading to the tree shaded **Battery Path**, past the elegant former French Mission Building which houses the **Court of Final Appeal** (no visitors), and on to ★★ **St John's Cathedral** ⑲ (open daily 7am–6pm).

Star Attractions
- **Bank of China Tower**
- **Hongkong Bank (HSBC)**
- **St John's Cathedral**

A regal touch
Guarding the Queen's Road entrance to the exceedingly modernistic Hong Kong Bank building are two bronze lions named Stephen and Stitt after former bank employees. As with most major accessories in Hong Kong, the silent sentinels help to ensure the bank good *fung shui*. Cast in England, the duo made it to Hong Kong for the unveiling of a 'new' Art Deco headquarters building back in 1935, and have perched in their current position since June 1985.

Interior, St John's Cathedral

Map
on pages
24–25

Japanese remodelling
During World War II Government House became the home of the Japanese commandant, who had it remodelled. At this time, the curious tower, which has a vague Shinto look about it, was added.

Those who built what is thought to be the oldest Anglican church in East Asia (consecrated in 1849, with a corner stone laid in 1847) could not decide between neo-Gothic and Norman styles, so settled on a mixture of the two, using local materials. During the Japanese occupation, the church was turned into a dance hall – a stark contrast to the current peaceful interior, with timbered ceiling and gently whirring fans.

From St John's, you can walk up Garden Road to Upper Albert Road for a peek through the gates of **Government House**, home to 25 British governors from 1855 to 1997. It is now used to receive the Special Administrative Region's official guests, and is open for public viewing four times a year (tel: 2530 2003).

GREEN EXPANSE

On the other side of Upper Albert Road lies another slice of colonial history, the ★★ **Hong Kong Zoological and Botanical Gardens** ❿ (daily 6am–7pm; free). Although small by international standards, it offers a pleasant green retreat from the city bustle, right in the heart of it all. The British established botanical gardens in all their colonies to provide facilities for research into the local flora; this one was opened in 1864. The gardens, with some 1,000 plant species from tropical and subtropical habitats, are a popular destination for family outings.

Lush greenery at the Zoological and Botanical Gardens

The small zoo was added in 1975, featuring an expansive display of birds alongside a decent collection of primates and reptiles. For easiest pedestrian access to the zoo, stroll five minutes across Caine Road from the outdoor escalator. The hike up Garden Road is a steep one, so be prepared to sweat, or hop in a cab.

HONG KONG PARK

Opened in 1991, nearby ★★ **Hong Kong Park** ❾ (daily 6.30am–11pm) offers another refreshing green space in the heart of the city. On the way the route passes the lower terminus of the **Peak**

Tram *(see page 49)*. The high-tech 32,300sq-ft (3,000sq-m) **Edward Youde Aviary** (daily 9am–5pm; free) houses magnificent brightly coloured birds from the Malaysian rainforest and other parts of Asia. Plant-lovers will head for the greenhouses of the **Forsgate Conservatory** (daily 9am–5pm; free), but the paths leading past the waterfalls also make an attractive walk.

If you're feeling energetic, you can climb the 105 steps of the 96-ft (30-m) observatory tower for a sweeping view of the park. Children are catered to with an expansive playground, and a new modern Thai restaurant and bar, called **L16** (tel: 2522 6333), offers al fresco dining within Hong Kong Park.

FLAGSTAFF HOUSE

The park site used to be known as Victoria Barracks, and inside, **Flagstaff House** was the residence of the British military commander until 1978. This whitewashed house was completed in 1846, originally built for Major General George Charles D'Aguilar, in the neo-Grecian manner and is one of Hong Kong's oldest surviving colonial buildings. Today, it houses the ★ **Museum of Tea Ware** ㉒ (daily except Tuesday and some public holidays 10am–5pm; free), for the viewing of centuries of Chinese tea culture.

Star Attractions
● **Hong Kong Zoological and Botanical Gardens**
● **Hong Kong Park**

Below: conservatory, Hong Kong Park
Bottom: Flagstaff House

Map below

Sightsee on board a tram

3: Wanchai to Causeway Bay

Trams – Pacific Place – Hung Shing Temple – Pak Tai Temple – Hong Kong Convention and Exhibition Centre – Happy Valley Race Course – Hong Kong Racing Museum – Noon Day Gun – Victoria Park – Tin Hau Temple

Hong Kong's traditional means of public transport, the tram, makes for an interesting – not to mention leisurely – alternative sightseeing tour of the city and its crowds. After rattling along between the daily bustle of businessmen in Central, housewives in Wanchai and shoppers in Causeway Bay, visitors can do their own shopping, relax in a park or visit a temple. Depending on where you decide to get off the tram and wander, this tour can take up to half-a-day.

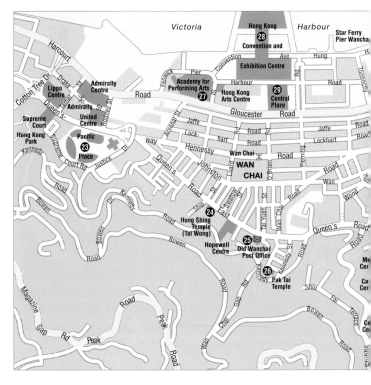

ELECTRIC TRAMS

Introduced in 1904, Hong Kong's fleet of 141 ★electric trams has remained virtually unchanged since the introduction of the familiar double-decker cars in 1925, apart from the recent modernisation of a handful of trams with new seats and air-conditioning. Redecorated annually according to advertising-agency whim, the trams run along the northern coast of Hong Kong Island daily from 6am until midnight.

The main line heads east from Central along Queensway, through Johnston Road to Hennessy Road and then past Victoria Park to King's Road. Going east, look for trams to 'North Point' or 'Shau Kei Wan'. A branch leads off through Percival Street to Happy Valley to the terminus south of the famous race course. Westbound trams are signed 'Western Market' and 'Kennedy Town'.

Ding-ding!

Hong Kong's trams — known locally as the 'ding-ding' for the bells that announce their arrival — offer one of the city's best bargains: an unlimited ride for HK$2, To ride the tram — jam packed at rush hour — enter through the turnstiles at the rear and gradually work up to the front. Deposit HK$2 near the driver upon disembarking, or use an Octopus stored-value card (see page 118).

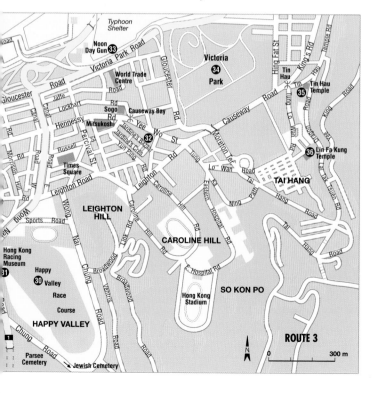

Map
on pages
40–41

Below: Pacific Place
Bottom: mirror-clad exterior
of Lippo Centre

Admiralty

Heading east from Central District the tram bumps past Statue Square, Legco Building, the Hongkong Bank (HSBC) headquarters and the Bank of China. Next on the left is the many-sided mirrored facade of the **Lippo Centre** (formerly the Bond Centre, after the bankrupted Australian financial speculator Alan Bond), now owned by an Indonesian industrial and banking group.

Then come **Admiralty Centre** and **United Centre**, two mixed-use office and shopping complexes. Opposite is the city's **Supreme Court**, followed by a newer multi-functional shopping centre worthy of superlatives: **Pacific Place** ㉓ (1990). The lower levels are filled with shops, restaurants, Asian fast-food outlets and pubs, plus an ice-skating rink and a four-auditorium cinema complex for English-language films. Above lies 5½ million sq ft (½ million sq m) divided among offices and three upmarket business hotels. There are also escalators leading directly up to **Hong Kong Park** *(see page 38)*, and a link to the Admiralty MTR station.

Wanchai and Queen's Road East

Past Pacific Place, the tram enters **Wanchai**. The new high-rent residential buildings of Star Crest are tucked into the hillside on the right, with

upmarket bars and restaurants below. For a more traditional side of the district, disembark to make a detour up **Queen's Road East**, marking Wanchai's original waterfront. Furniture shops offer rattan sofas and rosewood dining tables and chairs. The ★ **Hung Shing (Tai Wong) Temple** ❷ on the right has a boulder incorporated into its design and a sacred banyan tree behind.

The circular **Hopewell Centre** (1980) was once the tallest building in Hong Kong, at 705ft (215m). For a spectacular view, take the glass bubble lift between the 17th and 56th floors.

The ★ **Old Wanchai Post Office** ❷ (1912–13) was in operation until 1992. It now houses an **Environmental Resource Centre** (Monday to Saturday 10am–5pm, Wednesday 10am–1pm) and many of its original fittings have been preserved.

One block down, **Stone Nullah Lane** on the right leads to an 1860s ★ **Pak Tai Temple** ❷ with a 10-ft (3-m) copper image of the Taoist god, made in 1604. Previously, visitors could witness traditional Taoist funeral ceremonies here, complete with the burning of elaborate paper offerings for the deceased to use in heaven – from entire houses and a quarter-sized Mercedes-Benz, to servants carrying trays of food. But sadly, recent decrees by the Chinese Temples Society have forbade such 'old-fashioned' practices, and it is unclear whether the tradition will survive.

WANCHAI WATERFRONT

The Queen's Road East area feels centuries apart from the modern structures that cluster on the reclaimed land along today's waterfront. Since 1985, the highly-regarded ★ **Hong Kong Academy For Performing Arts (APA)** ❷ has trained students in drama, music, dance and stage technique. Simon Kwan, the architect who designed the building, has accentuated the unusual ground plan with the frequent use of triangles.

Opposite lies the **Hong Kong Arts Centre** which includes a theatre, a cinema and galleries. Further east, sandwiched between the Grand Hyatt and Renaissance Harbour View hotels, is

> ### Harbour views
> To detour over to the convention centre and waterfront area, take the covered walkway from Hennessy Road near Wanchai MTR exits A1, A2 or A4. The walkways are signed all the way through Central Plaza and on to the Hong Kong Convention and Exhibition Centre (HKCEC). The **Expo Promenade** outside affords one of the best skyline views of both Hong Kong Island and Kowloon, with a pleasantly landscaped sitting-out area. Though some may find the towering Golden Bauhinia statue a bit garish, it does commemorate the return of the former British colony to the People's Republic of China.

Chinese opera actor applying make-up

Map
on pages
40–41

the ★ **Hong Kong Convention and Exhibition Centre ㉘**. Its low-rise extension jutting out into the harbour was completed in 1997, just in time to host the historic Handover Ceremony in which Britain formally returned Hong Kong to China at midnight on 30 June. Behind the convention centre is Hong Kong's tallest building, **Central Plaza ㉙** (1992), which at 1,227ft (374m) is now the world's fifth highest.

TO HAPPY VALLEY

Back on the tram, the tracks fork right off Hennessy Road onto **Johnston Road**, another Wanchai street that has managed to retain some of its original character. Look out for a group of three narrow colonnaded 'shop-houses', once typical but now rare, and the traditional markets in the side streets on the right. Bargain shoppers will appreciate the several stores along Johnston Road, between Luard and Fleming roads, that sell overruns of designer-brand Western fashions at discounted prices.

The tram then rejoins **Hennessy Road**, the main thoroughfare between Wanchai and Causeway Bay. A typical combination of offices and shops continues along both sides of the street. Trams marked **Happy Valley** turn right along **Percival Street**, where shops selling electronics

Below: exhibit, Hong Kong Racing Museum
Bottom: Happy Valley Race Course

and Chinese medicines stand cheek by jowl, before turning into Wong Nai Chung Road, wrapping around the race course to the Happy Valley terminus. Either continue on foot or climb into the front tram and wait for it to move off again.

AT THE RACES

The **Happy Valley Race Course** ❸⓪ was established in 1846 in a lush rice-growing valley unsuitable for settlement due to malarial mosquitoes. Today, the track is surrounded by high-rises and has the state-of-the-art ★**Hong Kong Racing Museum** ❸① (Tuesday to Sunday and public holidays 10am–5pm; race days 10am– 12.30pm; free) which traces the history of the sport.

Wednesday evening races from September to June are packed with local residents, the majority of whom come for the gambling rather than the horses. General admission costs HK$10. Betting on horse races is the only legalised form of gambling in Hong Kong, and brings in more than HK$91 million a year.

SHOPS GALORE

Back on Hennessy Road in Causeway Bay, the tram passes **Mitsukoshi** and **Sogo**, large Japanese department stores which, along with the massive **Times Square** mall and countless shops in between, contribute to the shopping mania of Causeway Bay. If you dislike crowds, this is no place to be on a weekend.

In the small, jam-packed shopping lanes of **Jardine's Bazaar** ❸② and **Jardine's Crescent**, there is plenty of cheap clothing and fresh foods for sale. The street names honour William Jardine, a trader who was one of the economic founders of the colony. With his partner, James Matheson, he established one of the most influential trading houses in Hong Kong. The company – which exists till today – still plays an important role in the commercial life of the city, and it is appropriate that the streets named after him should be as business-inclined.

> ### Cemetery stories
> The Happy Valley cemeteries on the opposite side of Wong Nai Chung Road, behind the race course, provide further insight into Hong Kong's colonial history. The lush green Parsee Cemetery, beside the Hindu temple to the south, is the most picturesque. Older headstones in the Hong Kong ('Colonial') Cemetery tell of early settlers' often premature deaths, while Portuguese memorials in St Michael's Roman Catholic Cemetery highlight the link with nearby Macau.
>
> There are surprisingly many Chinese names listed in the Muslim Cemetery, from where you can look down onto the back of a 19th-century Sikh Temple. The memorials to many prominent Hong Kong citizens in the Jewish Cemetery are worth a detour up Shan Kwong Road.

Times Square

Military insights

Over a century ago, the British built the Lei Yue Mun Fort to protect the eastern approach to Victoria Harbour. In July 2000, the **Hong Kong Museum of Coastal Defence** (Friday to Wednesday 10am–5pm; admission fee) opened at the restored fort – an unusual setting with historical connections. Exhibits are centred in the Redoubt, showcasing 600 years of coastal defence in southern China, from the Ming dynasty through the 1997 Handover. Included are informative videos on the Opium Wars and the Japanese invasion of Hong Kong in 1941. An historical trail leads down to the exit, passing gun emplacements and old barracks, with spectacular views over the harbour.

Allow more than one hour to visit the museum. To get there, take the MTR to Shau Kei Wan (east of Causeway Bay), exit at B2 and follow the signs (a 15-minute walk). On weekends, there's a free shuttle bus from the Heng Fa Chuen MTR station.

NOON DAY GUN

The firm of Jardine Matheson also owns the ★ **Noon Day Gun** ㉝, which is fired punctually every day (and was immortalised in the song 'Mad Dogs and Englishmen' by Noel Coward). It stands by the Typhoon Shelter near the Excelsior Hotel. The safest way to cross the multi-lane carriageway is via a tunnel, accessible from the entrance to the World Trade Centre. The origins of the gun are somewhat obscure, although it is known that the opium traders had their own cannon and ammunition stores and were accustomed to greeting their *taipans* – the equivalent of today's senior board members – with a welcoming salvo as their ships entered harbour.

According to one legend, the ritual began in the mid-1800s when one of Jardine's opium boats sailed into the harbour and was given a 21-gun salute. The navy, however, considered the privilege should be reserved for its senior officers and ordered Jardine Matheson to use up its remaining ammunition by firing a shot every day at noon. Until 1960, a six-pounder rang out across the harbour, but people found it too loud, so Jardines halved the calibre.

VICTORIA PARK

Passengers continuing east on the tram will see a newly renovated **Victoria Park** ㉞ on their left. An unsmiling statue of the queen sits halfway along the street boundary. Locals use the park for *tai chi*, walks and outings with the children, while the part closest to Causeway Bay is the meeting place for Indonesian domestic helpers on Sunday, their day off. There are asphalt football pitches as well as basketball, tennis and squash courts, a small roller skating arena, swimming pool and jogging trail. During the Lantern Festival, parents and children come to picnic under the full moon with their elaborate lanterns.

The park hosts a flower market in the week before Chinese New Year, as well as a week-long flower show every March. Opposite the park and visible to the right side of Causeway Road is Hong

Kong's new **Central Library**, a massive yellow eyesore built in a mishmash of architectural styles.

TIN HAU TEMPLE

Leave the tram just after the park and walk to the right, up Tin Hau Temple Road. The ★ **Tin Hau Temple** ❸❺ (one of several found in Hong Kong) is perched on a granite ledge about a hundred yards along. During the 18th century, when this area was still right on the waterfront, the inhabitants of the bay erected a temple in honour of the Taoist Queen of Heaven and patron goddess of fishermen and sailors. It is a simple building painted predominantly in red, the colour of good fortune. Elderly neighbourhood women come to lay their offerings before the statue of Tin Hau on the central altar and to pay respect to their ancestors in the little room on the right.

Below: fortune sticks
Bottom: Tin Hau temple

It's easy to return to your hotel from here, as the Tin Hau MTR station is just across King's Road. Aternatively, turn left on Tung Lo Wan Road and walk five minutes (past the Metropark Hotel) to reach **Lin Fa Kung Temple** ❸❻, dedicated to the Goddess of Mercy. With an octagonal structure in the front and a massive boulder that now forms part of the architecture, this 1864 temple, most recently renovated in 2002, is one of Hong Kong's most unusual Buddhist shrines.

Map below

4: Victoria Peak

The Peak – Peak Tram – Lugard Road – Pinewood Battery – Peak Tower

Expect panoramic views from Victoria Peak

The world-famous panorama from The Peak should be included in every visitor's itinerary. The journey to the top by the Peak Tram is an experience in itself. From the observation pavilion or the viewing terrace at the Peak Tower, visitors can gaze down on the jungle of skyscrapers and (on a clear day at least), the busy harbour and Kowloon Peninsula over to the Nine Dragon Ridge, which separates metropolitan Hong Kong from the New Territories.

At night the area becomes a dazzling spectacle of lights. A gentle stroll on the level path surrounding The Peak will take about an hour before dinner (you'll probably need insect repellent).

THE PEAK

★★★ **Victoria Peak** ❸❼ (more popularly referred to as the Peak), at 1,817ft (554m), the highest point on the island, was settled from the 1870s onwards on the advice of the chief medical officer of the colonial administration. The European

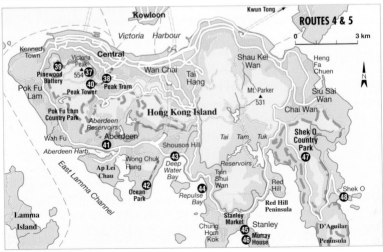

residents wanted to escape from the densely built-up Western District and initially reserved the slopes facing the harbour for themselves. But transport up the steep slopes proved extremely tiresome, particularly as the Europeans were accustomed to being carried home in sedan chairs by coolies – a highly uncomfortable experience for all concerned in view of the uneven paths and heartstoppingly steep incline.

Star Attractions
● Views from Victoria Peak
● Peak Tram

PEAK TRAM

It was not until the ★★★ **Peak Tram** ㊳ made its first journey in May 1888 that the Peak really came into its own and colonial villas began appearing on the airy heights. Until the completion of the Peak road in 1924, the tram was the only mechanical means of transport on the mountain. The tram is really a funicular railway and its two carriages are linked by a steel cable, so that the downhill tram partly helps to pull the other one in an uphill direction by its own weight. In 1926, the steam engine was replaced by an electric one, and larger Swiss-built carriages with electronic controls, accommodating 120 passengers, are now in use.

The No 1 green minibus provides an alternative means of reaching the top. It leaves from Lung Wui Road to the east of City Hall in Central and scales the once inaccessible heights via Magazine Gap Road. The first road link was Stubbs Road, named after the governor of the time. The double-decker bus No 15 from Exchange Square also affords fine views of the city and the elegant villas. The residences of a number of consulates can be distinguished by the fluttering flags outside. Two good spots for a view of the city and harbour are the terrace on Level 5 of the Peak Tower and the little observation pavilion to the east on narrow Findlay Road.

Bus alternative
For anyone who finds the Peak Tram too steep, there are plenty of leisurely buses, all of which offer spectacular views, that reach the Peak from all over town: the No 15C from the Star Ferry in Central, No 12S from Admiralty, No 15 from Exchange Square, No 15B from Tin Hau and No 515 from Sai Wan Ho on eastern Hong Kong Island.

Ride the Peak tram

LUGARD ROAD STROLL

At this altitude there is usually at least a tepid breeze encouraging the visitor to make the 3-kilometre circuit of the summit on foot. The narrow

Map on page 48

Over the top
Getting up to the highest point of the mountain is worth the effort – head straight up Mount Austin Road. There is no public transport, but you can take a taxi. Expensive private residences line the narrow road to the summit, where taxi drivers often appear after hours with girlfriends or wives in tow, as the view from here by night is unparalleled. Just below the lookout area sprawls the tropical Victoria Peak Garden. This is one of the most pleasant, grassy hillside spots for a picnic on Hong Kong Island.

Peak Lookout café

★ **Lugard Road** starts directly opposite the **Peak Tower** tram terminus building, and offers a fresh perspective at every bend. When the city disappears from sight, the islands of Lantau and Lamma appear on the horizon away to the west, while to the south the sun is reflected in the glittering South China Sea. The tree-lined path winding past isolated villas feels a world apart from the bustling metropolis below.

More than halfway around the loop, Lugard Road merges with **Harlech Road** at a junction and shady picnic spot. Continue east until the path brings you back to the start. From here, **Mount Austin Road** climbs steeply to the real summit, which affords magnificent views.

PINEWOOD BATTERY

History buffs can pay a visit to an old battery located halfway down the Peak. Where Lugard Road meets Harlech Road, veer onto Harlech and immediately onto Hatton Road, following the signs downhill to Pinewood Battery and the Morning Trail. About 15 minutes beyond lie the ruins of ★ **Pinewood Battery** ㊆, an excellent lookout point above Western District. Originally built to repel possible attacks by the Russians or French, the fortifications were upgraded prior to World War II. Today, the place affords relative peace and quiet above the city. The battery is also a pleasant place to watch the sun set.

Either return to the Peak from here, or continue downhill to the end of Hatton Road, and cross over to Kotewall Road, near the gates of Hong Kong University. From here, bus No 13 leads back to the Central Star Ferry.

PEAK DINING

Those in need of refreshments will find several choices on the Peak. Two of the nicest are the **Peak Lookout** (tel: 2849 1000) – formerly the Peak Café – housed in a former shelter for sedan chair bearers, and **Café Deco** (tel: 2849 5111) in the Peak Galleria. It's a good idea to book ahead on weekends and holidays. Both feature a range of foods, from Southeast Asian specialities to fresh oysters and imported steaks. The Peak Lookout's patio is pleasant year-round; during the winter months, sophisticated gas lamps are fired up to repel the damp chill of the mountain air.

Those wanting a quick snack or a light bite can nip into Grappa's Deli for Italian, EAT Noodles, the Pacific Coffee Company (with a fabulous view) or the Haagen-Daz ice-cream café.

PEAK TOWER AMUSEMENTS

Other amusements on offer at **Peak Tower** **40** are the **Ripley's Believe It or Not! Odditorium** (daily 9am–10pm; admission fee), complete with a real shrunken human head and headless hen, and themed virtual reality rides at the **Peak Explorer Motion Simulator**.

The latest attraction in Peak Tower is **Madame Tussaud's Hong Kong** (daily 11am–8pm; admission fee), with more than 100 lifelike wax statues of celebrities, including actors like Bruce Lee, Jackie Chan and Michelle Yeoh, and Chinese president Jiang Zemin.

The exhibit is decidedly hands-on, so bring a camera and pose alongside your favourite star. Souvenir shopping in the Peak Galleria provides an alternative to all this activity.

Below: exhibit at Ripley's
Bottom: Peak Tower at night

Map
on page
48

5: South Side

Aberdeen – Ocean Park – Repulse Bay – Stanley Market – Murray House – Shek O

While the north coast of Hong Kong is gradually being extended by a succession of land reclamation schemes, the south is characterised by long peninsulas, little bays with beaches, offshore islands and an almost resort-like atmosphere. Of course, there are high-rises here too, but the visitor will discover numerous other gems. The complete tour of the south will take at least a day, but one can return to the city at any point.

ͰͰͰ Chinese furniture

Those seeking more shopping action should head for the warehouses full of antique Chinese furniture and home décor at Hing Wai Centre (7 Tin Wan Praya Road) in Aberdeen and Horizon Plaza (2 Lee Wing Street) in Ap Lei Chau, just south of Aberdeen. From Causeway Bay, take bus No 671 (in front of Mitsukoshi) directly to Horizon Plaza.

ABERDEEN HARBOUR

Buses No 7 and 71 run from Central (near the Outlying Islands Ferry Pier) through the Western District along the coast to Pokfulam and then to **Aberdeen**. Named after a British foreign secretary in the 1840s, Aberdeen is one of the oldest settlements in Hong Kong. Indeed, its Chinese name, Heung Gong Tsai ('Little Fragrant Harbour') is thought to be the origin of the whole territory's name.

Follow Aberdeen Main Road down to the ★ **Aberdeen Harbour** ㊶. Although most descendants of Aberdeen's original Tanka and Hoklo

Chaotic Aberdeen waterfront

'boat people' now live in the surrounding high-rises, this is still one of Hong Kong's liveliest waterways. A *sampan* (small boat) ride through Aberdeen Harbour is a highlight. The *sampan* operators (often surprisingly elderly women) are happy to negotiate a fee for a quick, occasionally hair-raising spin between fishing trawlers, ramshackle live-aboard junks, yachts and other craft.

The kitschy **Jumbo Floating Restaurant** (tel: 2873 7111) and sister establishments are an attraction in their own right, particularly when illuminated at night. Get there by free shuttle boat. Be warned, however, that most Hong Kong residents consider meals at Jumbo to be rip-offs of equally large proportions.

OCEAN PARK

Lying on a narrow peninsula just south of Aberdeen is ★★**Ocean Park** ❷ (www.oceanpark.com.hk; daily 10am–6pm; admission fee), billed as Southeast Asia's largest amusement and entertainment centre. Don't miss the cable car ride over the headland to the park's highlights, including the stunning **Pacific Pier** (showcasing seals and sea lions in their natural habitat); **Atoll Reef** and **Shark Aquarium**; 360-degree views from the 236ft (72m) observation tower; and the **Raging River** adventure ride. The **Middle Kingdom** section traces 5,000 years of Chinese history through cultural shows, artisan workshops and architectural reproductions.

Two giant pandas given by Beijing, An An and Jia Jia, reside in a HK$80 million air-conditioned habitat. To reach the park from Aberdeen, take a No 90, 96 or 107 bus; the No 629 bus offers a direct service from the Star Ferry in Central and Admiralty MTR station.

Bus No 73 continues along the coast from Aberdeen (from Ocean Park's Wong Chuk Hang Road exit, take the southbound No 73, 6A or 260). The first port of call is **Deep Water Bay** ❸, an address favoured by Hong Kong residents who can afford to build spacious villas on unobstructed slopes. Opposite the little beach lies the small but

Star Attraction
● Ocean Park

Below: 'sampan' operator
Bottom: cable cars over Ocean Park

Map
on page
48

Below: Repulse Bay condo with 'hole' in its middle
Bottom: beach fun at Repulse Bay

exclusive **Hong Kong Golf Course**. In the bay, a flotilla of yachts rest at anchor; they belong to the **Royal Hong Kong Yacht Club**, which has one of its three clubhouses on Middle Island, just a few yards from the shore.

REPULSE BAY

As the bus rounds the next headland, ★ **Repulse Bay ㊹** comes into view, dominated by a massive wall of condominiums built in the 80s. In the middle of its gently curving facade is a large rectangular space. The story has it that the developers left the space for good *fung shui* (so the mountain's 'dragon spirit' still had access to the sea).

The bus stops in front of **The Repulse Bay**, a replica of the colonial-style old Repulse Bay Hotel (1920), which was demolished to make way for the condo development. The original had been a summer resort popular among the colonial administrators and visiting celebrities such as the writer Graham Greene.

In its present incarnation as an upmarket restaurant and shopping complex, it is home to one of Hong Kong's most romantic European restaurants, the **Verandah** (tel: 2812 2722).

Repulse Bay, named after a 19th-century British warship involved in hunting local pirates, is the most famous bay in south Hong Kong. The beach has a wide range of amenities from changing rooms and showers to fast-food restaurants, and is crowded on weekends. One of its more curious attractions is the whimsical collection of Buddhist and Taoist statues that watch over the swimmers from the ★ **Life Guard Club** at the south end of the beach. The No 73 bus continues on to **Stanley** If you're re-boarding at Repulse Bay you can also take the No 6 and 260 buses on to this next destination.

STANLEY

Named after a British colonial minister, Stanley lies at the narrowest point on a long spit of land, the southern section of which is military property.

Disembark at the end of Stanley Village Road – ideally on a weekday, when there is not such a crowd – and join in the lively atmosphere of ★★ **Stanley Market** ㊺ (daily 11am–6pm). Prices are no longer as low as they once were, but the quality is better here than at the Temple Street Night Market. Good buys include beautifully embroidered household linens, silk clothing, international brand name 'seconds' and sports shoes.

Star Attractions
● Stanley Market
● Murray House

STANLEY BAY

Continue through the market towards the exit on **Stanley Main Street**, which overlooks Stanley Bay. Choose from a number of cafés with a view, such as The Boathouse on the corner, or continue on towards the mall complex of **Stanley Plaza**. The exterior is a pleasant sitting-out area for both visitors and residents of the relatively recently built Ma Hang Estate. Signs point in the direction of the tiny **Tai Wong Temple** built into a rock, the waterfront **Pak Tai Temple**, and the **Tin Hau Temple**, one of the oldest on Hong Kong Island.

Sitting square in the plaza and next to the Tin Hau Temple is another monument to Hong Kong's colonial history, ★★ **Murray House** ㊻. The colonial military barracks, dating to 1843, was dismantled in 1982 to make way for the Bank of China Tower in Central. After years in storage,

Stanley no more?
In 2002, residents of Stanley were informed of the possible razing of Stanley Market to make way for yet another shopping centre. It is hoped the plan will be rejected – but check with your hotel concierge before heading south.

Altar at Tai Wong Temple

Map on page 48

the Greek Revival-style building was reassembled on the Stanley waterfront. Interesting exhibits on the building's history are displayed downstairs, while restaurants are gradually filling in the upper floors.

The quickest way back to Central from Stanley is by bus No 6A, 6X or 260 via the tunnel route (for Tsim Sha Tsui, take No 973). The journey on to Shek O is more complicated as there is no direct public transport link; your best bet is simply to take a taxi. If you insist on public transport, take the No 14 bus towards Shau Kei Wan as far as the roundabout at Shek O Road, then switch to a No 9 bus towards Shek O.

A legacy from colonial days – Murray House

CAPE D'AGUILAR

Tai Tam Road follows the coast and affords fine views of the sea. It is not surprising, therefore, to find that the hillside below the road is dotted with houses which are only accessible from above. Then two huge tower blocks appear, one of them named after Hong Kong's rival in skyscraper construction, Manhattan. The residents enjoy splendid views which compensate for the long journey into town. There is an interesting housing estate on the **Red Hill Peninsula**, with exclusive Spanish-style terraced houses built on different levels, and ever more construction.

Tai Tam Road twists and turns to reach the roundabout mentioned earlier, at which point one can change to the No 9 bus. Just beyond (and heading back towards Shau Kei Wan) is the narrow wall surrounding the Tai Tam Tuk reservoir. In fact there are three interlinked reservoirs in all, surrounded by a network of country footpaths.

Shek O Road continues down to the **D'Aguilar Peninsula**, named after the first commander-in-chief of the British military forces in the new colony. Most of the peninsula is taken up by the ★ **Shek O Country Park** ㊼, which is crossed by a number of hiking routes, including the famous ★ **Dragon's Back ridge walk**. Further south is the relatively inaccessible **Cape D'Aguilar Marine Reserve**, recently found to be the territory's prime bird-watching site for seabirds during typhoons.

SHEK O

Shek O ㊸ is a curious village in which some families have lived for decades in modest homes next to the magnificent villas of wealthy neighbours. It is pleasant to stroll through the village streets to its little central square, where there is an attractive temple. The marketplace sells a selection of beach paraphernalia.

During the week, the beach is one of the quietest and most attractive on the island. The popular **Shek O Chinese-Thai Seafood** restaurant (daily 11am–10pm) stands by the roundabout at the entrance to the village and is reasonably priced. For a mellow café feel, try the bohemian-style **Black Sheep** (tel: 2809 2021; dinner daily from 6pm; lunch on weekends only). There are only nine tables at this long-standing restaurant, so reservations are recommended. Ingredients are fresh and tasty, and prices mirror those in Central, but the zesty mint lemonade is a godsend after the hike over the Dragon's Back.

Getting back to town is much easier. The No 309 bus runs directly to Exchange Square in Central, while the No 9 bus goes to Shau Kei Wan MTR station.

> **Hiking Dragon's Back**
> The Dragon's Back ridge *(see opposite)* runs at an average 600ft (200m) in height. There is usually a fresh breeze atop the mountains, and magnificent sea views. Pack drinking water and suntan lotion, as there are few shade-giving trees. The hike is relatively easy but does feature some short inclines. To get there, disembark from the No 9 bus along winding Shek O Road near Cape Collinson Road, at the entrance to Shek O Country Park, and follow the signs. Trail's end leads down paved steps back to Shek O Road. From here, catch a bus or taxi into Shek O.

Picturesque Shek O beach

Map opposite

Star Ferry

Before the Cross Harbour Tunnel opened in 1972, the Star Ferry was the only way across Victoria Harbour. Whether you were a fishmonger or tycoon, you had to take the ferry between Hong Kong Island and Kowloon. After more than 100 years of service, the Star Ferry still provides the cheapest, and certainly the most scenic, means of crossing Hong Kong's heart. Passengers over the age of 65 ride for free.

Kowloon's landmark Clock Tower

6: Kowloon

Clock Tower – Cultural Centre – Museum of Art – Space Museum – Nathan Road – Kowloon Park – Science Museum – Museum of History – Temple Street Night Market

Nathan Road seems to exert a magical attraction on the shoppers of this world. Every day, thousands of them throng in front of its shop windows and haggle over prices inside. But **Tsim Sha Tsui**, the tip of Kowloon Peninsula, is also home to museums and culture. Further up the peninsula, life remains more down-to-earth, with day markets selling everything one can possibly imagine and the famous Temple Street Night Market.

To do this tour justice, you'll need a full day. However, your proximity to public transport – MTR being the easiest – means you can pick and mix according to preference and time available.

CULTURAL CENTRE

Take note of the time by the **Clock Tower** ㊾ – the only remains of the original Kowloon-Canton Railway terminus – directly next to the Star Ferry Pier. Don't look for accuracy though, for the four clocks on the faces of the tower are not synchronised and therefore do not always show the same time. In 1975, the railway station was torn down and replaced by a modern building in Hung Hom but the clock tower, a relic dating from the Age of Steam, built in 1915 – was renovated and preserved. Where the tracks used to be, palm trees now frame a succession of interlinked pools.

The large bronze sculpture of the Flying Frenchman was created by the French artist Cesar Baldaccini (1921–98).

On the site of the former railway station, the tiled facade of the **Hong Kong Cultural Centre** ㊿ rises skywards. Officially opened in 1989, the centre houses two large concert halls and a studio theatre, all frequently used by the Hong Kong Philharmonic Orchestra and visiting performers. However, it is difficult to understand why the government permitted architect José Lee's almost windowless building on a site which enjoys one of the most magnificent views in the world.

THE WATERFRONT

Visitors can enjoy the view across to Hong Kong Island, however, by taking a stroll along the ★★**Waterfront Promenade** ⑤ – something which should be done at least twice during any stay in Hong Kong, once by day and once by night. The tips of the skyscrapers reaching out of the modern concrete jungle on the opposite side of the harbour soar ever higher, and with a bit of luck, a freighter will sail across the scene, framing the perfect view for photography.

In fact, local young enterprneuers have combined the fabulous view with high technology, setting up digital cameras on tripods to capture the moment for tourists and lovebirds in one of Hong Kong's most romantic settings. In a few minutes, they download the pictures to a laptop computer and print out quality photographs while you wait.

MUSEUM OF ART

The ★**Hong Kong Museum of Art** ⑤ (daily except Thursday and some public holidays, 10am–6pm; admission fee) stands directly on the waterfront. On show are pictures portraying Hong Kong as well as old Chinese works, a valuable collection of Chinese paintings and calligraphy, and classics by artists who belong to the contemporary Hong Kong School.

Since the beginning of the 20th century, this group has been searching for a synthesis of East and West, although for many years they were 'too Chinese' for the West and too modern for the Orient. Today, the reputation of their works as 'classics' is denied by no one. Admission is free every Wednesday.

Map on page 59

SPACE MUSEUM

The first museum in the cultural complex was established in 1980 on Salisbury Road. The egg-shaped ★ **Hong Kong Space Museum** ㉝ (Monday, Wednesday to Friday 1–9pm, Saturday, Sunday and public holidays 10am–9pm; children under 3 years not admitted; admission fee) is dedicated to the conquest of space and the exploration of the stars. Its high-tech **Space Theatre** planetarium features wide-screen Omnimax films and Sky shows several times each day.

'THE PEN'

On the other side of Salisbury Road stands ★★ **The Peninsula** ㉞, the grand dame of Hong Kong hotels. Opened on 11 December 1928, it was the first hotel on Kowloon, strategically positioned for passengers travelling overland to Europe by train. The Peninsula lobby became the favourite rendezvous for high society: to this day, guests sit beneath the gilt stucco ceiling to see and be seen. Afternoon high tea or evening cocktails to strains of the resident string orchestra are a wonderful way to recapture the atmosphere of a bygone age, but do pay attention to attire. The dress code has been relaxed until 6.30pm, but shorts and men's sandals are never welcome.

Modernists might prefer the Philippe Starck-designed **Felix** restaurant-cum-bar and nightclub (tel: 2315 3188) in the 30-storey extension tower. Although it recently won an award as one of the top restaurants worldwide, foodies agree that there is finer dining to be had in the territory, and often just stop by for a drink – and the view. Check out the avant-garde toilets at the end of the hall, too.

THE GOLDEN MILE

Exit via the Peninsula Shopping Arcade onto bustling **Nathan Road**, a canyon of neon lined with shops, hotels, restaurants and dubbed Kowloon's **'Golden Mile'**. Its early 20th-century nickname was 'Nathan's Folly', poking fun at the governor, Matthew Nathan, for building a wide

Strictly for bikers
To witness a rumble in this jungle of a city, wander down Ashley Road on a Sunday morning around 10am. The Hong Kong Harley Owners Group (HOG) chapter meets weekly to ride their Harley-Davidson bikes into the outer reaches of the territory. For more information, visit their website (www.H-O-G.org).

Lobby area of The Peninsula

tree-lined avenue on the almost unpopulated Kowloon Peninsula when the colony's social life centred almost exclusively on Hong Kong Island. Today, its teeming streets and forest of neon signs epitomise the visitor's conception of what Hong Kong must be like.

Just past the junction of Haiphong Road, on the left, is the modern **Kowloon Mosque**. This is the largest mosque in Hong Kong and the spiritual abode of some 50,000 Muslims. It stands on the site of a late 19th-century mosque built for Muslim troops stationed in the British army barracks at what is now **Kowloon Park** ㉟ (daily 6am–midnight). Inside the park, a few yards on the right, is a path leading to the sculpture garden where artists from Hong Kong and further afield display their work. Behind is the maze from which paths lead to the flamingo pool, children's playgrounds, pavilions and the formal gardens.

SCIENCE MUSEUM

From Kowloon Park, choose one of two options. The first is to cross Nathan Road and walk east along **Granville Road**, famous for its 'factory outlet' shops selling 'seconds' or over-runs of garments manufactured locally for export. There are still bargains to be had here, though the pickings are slimmer than they used to be. At the end of the

Star Attraction
● **The Peninsula**

Below: Kowloon Park
Bottom: Nathan Road shop

Map on page 59

⟡ Museum pass

Museum lovers may want to pick up a Museum Weekly Pass, which affords unlimited admission to the Hong Kong Museum of Art, Science Museum, Space Museum and Museum of History (all in Tsim Sha Tsui), the Heritage Museum (Sha Tin) and the Museum of Coastal Defence (eastern Hong Kong Island). The pass costs HK$30 and is available from all HKTB Visitor Information Centres. Admission to each museum is normally HK$10.

street, take the raised pedestrian walkway over Chatham Road South. Follow the signs to the ★ **Hong Kong Science Museum** ❺❻ (Monday to Wednesday, Friday 1–9pm; weekends and some public holidays 10am–9pm; admission fee) a wonderland of interactive, hands-on exhibits exploring the mysteries of science and technology.

MUSEUM OF HISTORY

Next door is the ★★ **Hong Kong Museum of History** ❺❼ (Monday, Wednesday to Saturday 10am–6pm; Sunday and public holidays 10am–7pm; admission fee). The museum recently relocated and unveiled its permanent exhibition, 'The Story of Hong Kong', in 2001, tracing the culture and history of Hong Kong from a peaceful rural backwater to a teeming metropolis. Reconstructed street scenes and interactive displays help ensure an enjoyable visit for all ages. Museum admission is waived every Wednesday.

KOWLOON STREET MARKETS

The second option on the tour takes in Kowloon's street markets. The nearest of these is the ★ **Jade Market** ❺❽ (daily 10am–3.30pm) on Kansu Street beneath the elevated road. Untreated and polished stones as well as finished items of jewellery are

Stones of every hue at the Jade Market

displayed in widely varying qualities. You are more likely to find an attractive souvenir than a valuable heirloom here.

Jade has a long history as a decorative stone in Chinese culture. It is usually green, occasionally white, and attracts extremely high prices throughout East Asia. Huge pieces weighing several tons can be seen adorned with delicate carvings of landscapes in temples and palaces. In Hong Kong, the superstitious use jade amulets to ward off evil spirits.

Star Attraction
● **Hong Kong Museum of History**

Below: Hong Kong Museum of History billboard
Bottom: Yau Ma Tei's Tin Hau Temple

TIN HAU TEMPLE

The best route to the Jade Market is from Yau Ma Tei MTR station (Man Ming Lane, exit C), turning right down Nathan Road and right again onto Public Square Street. This takes you past a little park and a quartet of temples named after the most famous of the four, the ★ **Tin Hau Temple ㊾**. Tin Hau, the patron goddess of fishermen and sailors, was the daughter of a fisherman who lived in Fujian Province on the coast of mainland China in the 13th century.

After she miraculously survived a tempest, Kublai Khan, the famous Mongol emperor proclaimed her as Tin Hau, or 'Queen of Heaven'. In the Taoist pantheon, Tin Hau ranks second only to the Jade Emperor. The Tin Hau Temple stands opposite the park entrance, with her statue against the far wall.

To the left of the Tin Hau Temple is a shrine to the city deity, Shing Wong. He ensures justice and law on earth and in the underworld and is thus accompanied by judges and soldiers. Further to the left, in the **Fok Tak Temple**, are a number of different deities, bearing witness to a strong element of religious tolerance as well as to a certain arbitrariness in the selection of gods.

To the right of the Tin Hau Temple, local gods are revered in the **Shea Tan Temple**, but the visitor will also re-encounter statues of Kwun Yum, Wong Tai Sin, Man, the God of Literature, and Mo, the God of War. Simple stones demonstrate that animist traditions are still very much alive.

Map on page 59

SHANGHAI STREET

The route continues through the neighbouring streets where the shops have been modernised, but where traditional wares are still on sale: temple goods such as statues of deities, candlesticks, incense sticks and sandalwood, and household items for the Chinese kitchen from woks and huge ladles to choppers and chopping boards.

Shanghai Street is full of shops which specialise in wedding attire. In former times, Chinese brides wore red – the colour of good fortune. The white worn by brides in the West, which is the Christian symbol of purity, symbolises mourning in China. Today, the displays along Shanghai Street are geared to both traditions.

Heads up
Be sure to keep close tabs on your wallet while wandering through the street markets. Although Hong Kong is a relatively safe place, pickpocketing is not unheard of – especially in crowded areas frequented by tourists.

LADIES' MARKET

At varying times of the day, food markets are set up along some of the streets in the neighbourhood, although their existence is threatened by the rapid changes taking place in the area. From Yau Ma Tei, one stop north on the MTR brings you to Mong Kok station. After taking the Nelson Street exit, continue past the first two intersections as far as **Tung Choi Street**. This is the scene of the busy ★**Ladies' Market** ⑩ (daily noon–10.30pm). A variety of clothing and shoes, household goods, jewellery and watches are displayed at the stalls.

Ladies' Market is renowned for bargain items

FISH, FLOWER & BIRD MARKETS

Continue north on Tung Choi Street, crossing busy Argyle Street and Mong Kok Road. This end of Tung Choi Street, known as **Goldfish Market** (10am–6pm), is where Hong Kong people buy the fish and aquariums considered lucky in *fung shui*. The parallel section of **Fa Yuen Street** (closest to Prince Edward MTR station) is known for its factory outlet shops and is a good place to pick up genuine fashion bargains.

At the north end of Fa Yuen Street, cross busy Prince Edward Road West, head one block east, take the first left into Sai Yee Street and first right into fragrant **Flower Market Road**, home to Hong

Kong's premier ★**Flower Market** ❻ (daily 10am–6pm). Show up around closing time to find some great bargains. At the far end you will find the **Yuen Po Street Bird Garden** (daily 7am–7pm).

For centuries, songbirds have been the most popular pets in Chinese households. Their owners take them for walks every day, carrying the cloth-covered cages through the streets and only removing the covers when they are hung up on trees in the park. Here, the birds entertain passers-by with a symphony of shrill arias.

As well as birds, you will find intricately-made cages for sale, and a selection of porcelain containers for food and water. There's also a lively trade in crickets, which are also kept by the Chinese as domestic musicians.

TEMPLE STREET NIGHT MARKET

Kowloon's most famous market, ★★**Temple Street Night Market** ❷ (best visited between 7pm and 10pm) runs three blocks west of Jordan MTR station (Exit A). Fabrics, leather goods, old posters of 'Shanghai girls', fake watches, dubious sex toys, electronic gadgets, CDs and videos – mostly cheap-label versions – are the main items on offer. Although everything is remarkably cheap, bargaining is an intrinsic part of the shopping experience.

Star Attraction
● Temple Street Night Market

Below and bottom: two markets with very different appeal: Temple Street Night Market and the Bird Market

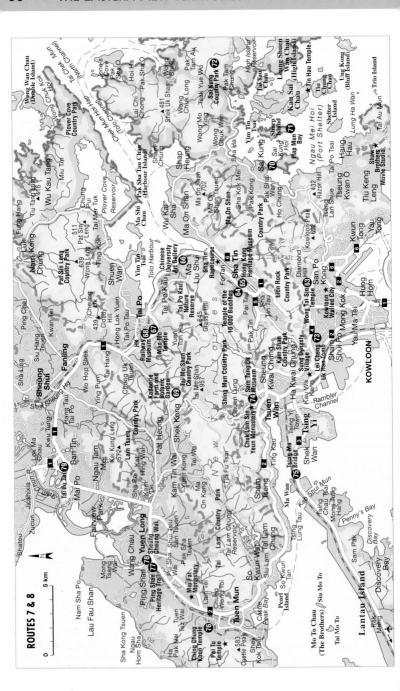

7: The Eastern New Territories

Wong Tai Sin Temple – Man Fat Tze – Heritage Museum – Sha Tin Race Course – Man Mo Temple – Railway Museum – Kadoorie Farm and Botanic Garden – Sai Kung

Concrete towers and housing blocks have replaced the muddy paddy fields of the New Territories. Visitors can combine their impressions of everyday life in suburban Hong Kong with a visit to several interesting temples or the excellent Heritage Musuem. The KCR overland railway provides rapid transportation north; allow a whole day for the trip. Alternatively, reach Sai Kung by MTR and bus to sample the seafood and go island hopping. Some may prefer to join a guided tour *(see text box page 81).*

WONG TAI SIN TEMPLE

The first stop should be at Hong Kong's most active, significant and wealthy temple, and the best place to get your fortune told. The ★★**Wong Tai Sin Temple** ⑬ (daily 7am–5.30pm; small donation expected) is signposted and easy to reach from Wong Tai Sin MTR station (exit B2).

According to legend, Wong Tai Sin was a shepherd boy from Zhejiang province. At age 15, an immortal taught him the art of transforming vermilion into a medicine which could heal all diseases. Also able to foretell the future, the miracle worker was revered as a demi-god after his death. Hong Kong residents visit the temple not only to beg for healing and ask for help with business problems, but also to have their futures prophesied. Within the temple compound is a large chemist's shop and one of Asia's largest concentrations of fortune tellers, who interpret the arcane texts which the faithful receive inside the temple.

Immigrants brought the first statue of Wong Tai Sin to Hong Kong in 1915 and placed it in a small temple in Wanchai. In 1921, his followers founded a charitable organisation known as Sik Sik Yuen, which moved the temple from crowded

Map on page 66

Star Attraction
● Wong Tai Sin Temple

Temple festival
To witness Wong Tai Sin Temple at its most lively and crowded, visit during the Chinese New Year festival or on the 23rd day of the eighth lunar month, which is the festival of Wong Tai Sin.

Praying for blessings – Wong Tai Sin Temple

Map on page 66

Wanchai to the then sparsely inhabited Kowloon. The 1920s building was demolished in 1968 and replaced by this impressive new complex, open since 1973.

TEMPLE INTERIOR

Below and bottom: Wong Tai Sin Temple's Nine Dragons Wall and altar table

The courtyard in front of the main temple – which combines the worship of Buddhist, Taoist and Confucian beliefs all at once – is on the left behind the imposing entrance door. Most of the worshippers in the courtyard are women, who make sacrifices all day or shake the bamboo spills for the fortune tellers. A picture of the Taoist deity can only be glimpsed at the far end of the ornate hall, which is almost always too crowded to cross.

On the right near the main hall stands the considerably smaller **Temple of the Three Saints**. These are Kwun Yum, the Goddess of Mercy, Kwan Ti, the God of War on the right, and Lü Dong Bin, one of the eight Taoist Immortals, on the left. In a neighbouring hall, the ancestral tablets of the deceased members of the Sik Sik Yuen are preserved. The next building is dedicated to Confucius.

Behind the temple and separate from it, lies the temple garden (daily 7am–5.30pm), which can only be reached through a single entrance. A particular attraction among the rocks, shrubs, streams and waterfalls is the **Long Walk** from the Summer Palace and the **Nine Dragons Wall** from the Imperial Palace in Beijing, which were copied here on a smaller scale.

SHA TIN

To reach the New Territories proper by MTR, travel two stations back to Yau Ma Tei and change to the KCR at Kowloon Tong. The train reaches hilly country after a few minutes and passengers may glimpse two famous rock formations on the right-hand side. **Lion Rock** is shaped like a lion's head, but **Amah (Mother) Rock** owes its name to a legend. A fisherman's wife waited for so long for her husband to return after a storm that she was turned to stone. (The Chinese are known for their imaginative interpretation of natural forms.)

The train quickly reaches **Sha Tin**, one of the New Towns that have sprung up since the 1970s in the New Territories, where more than 50 percent of Hong Kong's population lives. The shopping centre and the residential area of Sha Tin begin on the far side of the station. If time allows, plunge into the masses to see for yourself.

Star Attraction
● Man Fat Tze

MAN FAT TZE

The ★★ **Man Fat Tze** ④ or **Monastery of Ten Thousand Buddhas** (daily 9am–5pm) is at the top of 400 steps, and well-signposted from Sha Tin KCR station. There is an escalator for those not up to taking the stairs, but worshippers believe they will gain merit for rebirth by making the climb.

The monastery was founded in 1957 by the monk Yuet Kai, who died in 1965 at the age of 87. He had previously predicted that his body would not decompose if he were to be buried behind the temple in a crouching position. True enough, when his disciples exhumed the body eight months later, they found it still in good condition. They covered his corpse in gold leaf and placed it in a building on the second level.

The main prayer hall lies on the first level. The large Buddha statues on the main altar, together

> **Meritorious deeds**
> En route to Man Fat Tze is the Po Fook Ancestral Hall, opened in 1990. Thousands of urns containing the ashes of the dead are preserved in this Tang Dynasty-style mausoleum. In front of the complex is a narrow footpath leading to the steps which good Buddhists climb to reach the temple, thereby gaining merit for rebirth.

Monastery of Ten Thousand Buddhas

Map on page 66

Below: horse racing at Sha Tin Race Course
Bottom: Sha Tin train stop

with Kwun Yum, a healing goddess and the Ruler of Heaven and Earth, are surrounded by 12,800 smaller Buddha statues, all donated. Conspicuous are the brightly coloured concrete and plaster figures in the forecourt. The figures on each side represent the 18 *Luohan*, the most important disciples of the Buddha; in the central pavilion is a Fasting Buddha as well as the animal companions of wise men in Chinese mystic writings.

HONG KONG HERITAGE MUSEUM

Also in Sha Tin is the excellent ★ **Hong Kong Heritage Museum** ❻ (Monday, Wednesday to Saturday 10am–6pm, Sunday and most public holidays 10am–7pm; admission fee). Opened in December 2000, the enormous museum, built to reflect a traditional Beijing-style home with a courtyard, features hands-on exhibits that appeal especially to small children. Fishing and rice farming feature prominently in the 12 displays. From the Sha Tin KCR station, either walk 15 minutes to Man Lam Road, take the free shuttle bus on weekends, or hail a taxi.

SHA TIN RACE COURSE

A branch line of the KCR which only operates on racing days (usually Saturday) leads to the modern **Sha Tin Race Course**, worth the detour only if a race is on. Up to 80,000 spectators can follow the races through binoculars or on the huge video wall. The most important aspect, of course, is the betting, which here is fully computerised. People also come here to enjoy the **Penfold Park** bird sanctuary in the centre of the track (closed Monday and race days).

Get off at the next KCR station, University, and take the shuttle bus to the **Chinese University Art Gallery** ❻ (Monday to Saturday 10am–4.45pm, Sunday 12.30–5.30pm, closed some public holidays; free), which has a fine collection of paintings and calligraphy from Guangdong Province, 300 bronze seals from the Han-Dynasty period and earlier, and over 400 jade carvings.

TAI PO

Further north on the KCR, disembark at Tai Po Market station and take a taxi to the ★**Man Mo Temple** ❻ on Fu Shin Street. Like its namesake in Hollywood Road, the temple is dedicated to the God of Literature, Man, and the God of War, Mo. Inscriptions at the entrance of the temple, founded in 1892, indicate the individual roles of the deities: 'The God of Literature controls the sun and the moon' and 'The God of War controls the mountains and rivers'.

On the main altar, Man holds a paintbrush and a sceptre; the red-faced Mo holds a sword. Above the doors of the main hall on both sides of the inner courtyard are representations of bats, considered symbols of good luck in China, because in Chinese, the words for 'good luck' and 'bat' sound alike.

Fu Road, at the bottom of the street, leads round to the tiny **Hong Kong Railway Museum** ❻ (daily 9am–5pm; closed Tuesday and public holidays; free) at 13 Shung Tak Street.

The picturesque building, which looks more like a Chinese temple than a railway station, was the original Tai Po Market Railway Station that was built in 1913. There is an old-fashioned booking office with displays of memorabilia inside, and carriages of different periods stand outside the museum.

> **Market days**
> In front of the Man Mo Temple, the village continues tradition with a lively daily market, which was well known during the 17th century. The area's original inhabitants, mostly Tanka, once made a good living as pearl collectors in nearby Tolo Harbour. Look carefully at the produce being sold. You'll find fresh vegetables, herbs, bamboo shoots and wire baskets swarming with frogs.

Man Mo Temple deities

Map on page 66

KADOORIE FARM AND BOTANIC GARDEN

Garden lovers should visit the ★★**Kadoorie Farm and Botanic Garden** ❻❾ (tel: 2488 1371; daily 9.30am–5pm; phone in advance) at Pak Ngau Shek. From the KCR, disembark at Tai Po Market or Tai Wo station and take bus No 64K (20 minutes) or a taxi (HK$40) to the farm on Lam Kam Road. Kadoorie Farm and Botanic Garden (KFBG) initially focused on agricultural aid for Hong Kong's farmers but later turned its attention to wildlife conservation and education, when the number of farmers dwindled. Visits by school groups are common, but few Hong Kong residents know about the idyllic beauty and important work of the KFBG.

Blooming on the verdant hillsides are gardens of rare plants and native tree species, medicinal herbs, and many of the territory's 123 native orchid species. In the mountains are hiking trails, where the territory's large mammals, such as barking deer, wild pigs, Chinese porcupines and pangolin are frequently spotted. Contrary to popular belief, plenty of wildlife still remains in Hong Kong. You just have to know where to look.

Golfing diversion

Golfers might like to visit one of Hong Kong's most attractive public courses, the Jockey Club Kau Sai Chau Public Golf Course (1995), with its two 18-hole, ocean-view courses designed by Gary Player. Historically, the British Army had used the area for shelling practice. From Sai Kung pier, take the regular, 20-minute ferry to the northern part of Kau Sai Chau Island (HK$50 roundtrip). Prices for one round of golf range from HK$350–540, and a driving range is available.

SAI KUNG

For an alternative day-long excursion, head north and east to the ★**Sai Kung Peninsula** ❼❶, arguably the most attractive part of the New Territories. Hiram's Highway branches off Clear Water Bay Road to the town of **Sai Kung**, a traditional fishing community, which in itself makes for an interesting excursion. Golfers and windsurfers flock to Sai Kung, while masses of Filipino residents attend the El Shaddai worship services every Sunday. Take note of this fact, as return transportation on Sunday evening is hard to come by.

Take the MTR to Choi Hung station (exit B), than board green minibus No 1 or 1A to the waterfront terminus at Sai Kung. The journey from Central should take just under one hour.

The most intriguing part of the town is tucked away behind the **Tin Hau Temple** off Yi Chun

Surfing action at Sai Kung Peninsula

Street, though little of the 'old town' feel remains. Mostly three-storey buildings house several generations under one roof, with fish drying in the streets, laundry hanging out of the windows, and traditional noodle shops interspersed with the odd Western-style restaurant. Residents are accustomed to seeing foreigners wandering the narrow alleyways, so no one should give you a curious second glance.

FRESH SEAFOOD

Strolling along the Sai Kung waterfront, you will see plenty of junks at anchor in the harbour, and fishing boats that sporadically arrive to sell the catch of the day directly to the locals who crowd the docks expressly for this purpose. Off to the right stretch several seafood restaurants, unmistakable for the sea creatures swimming live in the tanks out front. Iridescent cuttlefish, metre-long reef fish and even horseshoe crabs make this an interesting – and educational – stop for families with children. Seeing a huge fish on the chopping block, however, may prove a bit more sobering. Bargain on the prices and be prepared to pay up.

For non-seafood meals, head to **Ali Oli Bakery** (where you can buy a good map) or the pricier **Jaspa's** in the centre of town. Around the corner, the unprepossessing **Chung Chuk Lam**

Below: fresh fish vendor
Bottom: Sai Kung is famous for its seafood restaurants

Map on page 66

Below: restaurant hostess
Bottom: hikers at Sai Kung

(tel: 2792 6883) serves up surprisingly good and very cheap Shanghainese fare. Raise a pint at Sai Kung's pubs **Poets**, **Cheers** and the **Duke of York**, or try **Steamers** for all-day breakfast, where the ladies lunch and the boys drink by night. Cap it all off with sweet Chinese dessert *(tangshui)* from **Honeymoon Dessert** on Po Tung Road (open 1pm–2am); ask for the English menu and try a 'Honeymoon Sweet Ball' with crushed peanuts and sesame inside.

ISLAND HOPPING

Along the waterfront, there's no escaping the lively little *sampan* ladies offering a quick spin around the harbour. Negotiate a hiring fee in advance. Larger boats too can ferry passengers to specific destinations, returning at the chosen time. Rates average about HK$100–200 per person for a couple of hours.

Favourite beach destinations are **Hap Mun Bay ❼**, complete with lifeguards, fishnets and crowds, and quieter **Pak Sha Beach** (Whiskey Beach) and **Kau Sai Wan Beach**, both *sans* shark nets but with cooling waters and white sand. Near the latter beach is the newly restored but charismatic **Hung Shing Temple ❼** (1889), dedicated to the God of the Sea. A model of a dragon boat is displayed in the main hall, and only a few houses make up this tiny village. Stopping off here will only take 10 minutes, but it is the journey around the islands that makes it so fascinating.

SAI KUNG HIKING

Relatively fit visitors who can handle steep climbs with stunning, panoramic ocean views should hike into the **Sai Kung Country Park ❼**, which stretches eastward from Sai Kung proper. Allow the better part of a day for the following hike.

From Sai Kung, take the snaking, 20-minute taxi ride to Sai Wan Pagoda (HK$90). Follow the paved path on the left, marked 'Sai Wan'. After a 30-minute up-and-down hike comes beautiful **Sai Wan Beach**. Just be wary of the strong undercurrent. There's no need to fear the friendly village dogs ambling along; they are always happy for a handout.

Continuing on, a path to the left of the footbridge follows a stream over rocky terrain to a secluded waterfall, reached after 20 minutes of scrambling. Bring a picnic lunch, drinking water and a swimsuit, and be sure to pack garbage out of the park.

HAM TIN

Back down at the concrete footbridge, continue across and follow signs towards **Ham Tin**, where a spectacular beach opens up after a steep downhill climb on Lilliputian paved steps. The scenery is overwhelmingly beautiful and stands in stark contrast to the 'other side' of Hong Kong.

At Ham Tin, a few restaurants serve fried rice, Singaporean noodles and iced lemon tea. From here the steep up-and-down trail leads over **Tai Long Au**. Once you have crossed over the highest point, follow the first set of steps down to the right, toward the ferry pier near **Sha Tau**. Hire a boat to **Wong Shek** (HK$20 per person), then take a public bus or taxi back into **Sai Kung**. Do remember to bring sunscreen and drinking water, and start early, as the sun sets year-round in Hong Kong no later than about 6.30pm.

> **Hiking heaven**
> Sai Kung Country Park is the starting point for the MacLehose Trail, which stretches for 60 miles (100 kilometres) through mostly open country, from one side of the New Territories to the other, across the hills as far as Tuen Mun. The trail is well-marked and there are places to camp along the way. Some parts are extremely steep and hard going but anyone who is used to hiking should have no problems tackling the shorter sections or any of the walks in this area.

A picturesque bay at Sai Kung Peninsula

Map on page 66

Flying high
Architects and engineers might like to detour from the traditional and learn more about the Hong Kong International Airport. From Tsuen Wan MTR station, take a No 96M maxicab to Ting Kau to see the **Airport Core Programme Exhibition Centre** (Tuesday to Friday 10am–5pm; weekends and some holidays 10am–6.30pm). As well as airport-related exhibits, the centre offers good views of the Tsing Ma Bridge, at 1.4 miles (2.2km), the world's longest road-and-rail suspension bridge.

Sam Tung Uk Museum

8: The Western New Territories

Lei Cheng Uk Tomb – Sam Tung Uk Museum – Tsing Ma Bridge – Ching Chung Koon Monastery – Ping Shan Trail – Tai Fu Tai

Central Hong Kong prides itself on its modernity. Until recently, even early colonial buildings were torn down without a second thought. But a wind of change is blowing through the skyscrapers. In the New Territories, with the assistance of village residents, ambitious restoration schemes are being undertaken to preserve the remains of the old Chinese inheritance in the region. In view of the somewhat complicated transport connections, an entire day should be set aside for exploring the western New Territories. Or simplify your life by joining a guided tour *(see box page 81)*.

LEI CHENG UK HAN TOMB

The fact that Hong Kong was settled during the Han Dynasty some 2,000 years ago (25–220AD) is proved by the existence of the ★ **Lei Cheng Uk Han Tomb** ❼ (Monday to Wednesday, Friday and Saturday 10am–1pm, 2–6pm; Sunday and public holidays 1–6pm; admission fee). The tomb was discovered during construction work in the Sham Shui Po District in 1955. The cross-shaped vault, made of bricks, was built without the use of mortar. Inside the grave, 58 pottery and bronze funerary offerings were found, copies of everyday objects which were intended to accompany the deceased beyond the grave. But neither body nor skeletal remains were found.

Today, visitors can peer into the vault and study the grave offerings in the on-site museum. The tomb rests in the middle of a public housing estate at 41 Tonkin Street, four blocks north of the **Cheung Sha Wan** MTR station (exit A3).

SAM TUNG UK MUSEUM

For more traditional Chinese culture and history, continue by MTR to **Tsuen Wan Station**, and follow the signs from exit E to the ★★★ **Sam Tung Uk Museum** ⓻ (Wednesday to Monday 9am–5pm; closed Tuesday and some public holidays; admission fee) on Kwu Uk Lane. This small walled village, whose name translates as 'three-beamed dwelling', was founded by the Chans, a Hakka family, in 1786, and is now dwarfed by high-rise housing estates. On display is period furniture and farming implements, and exhibitions on Chinese folk culture.

Another traditional Hakka dwelling, the ★ **Hoi Pa Village Old House** (1904), survives as an Environmental Resource Centre in the lovely, almost imperial-styled **Jockey Club Tak Wah Park** off Tsuen Wan Market Street, a five-minute walk from the MTR station.

CHING CHUNG KOON MONASTERY

Out of the way but interesting is the Ching Chung Koon Monastery in **Tuen Mun**. From Tsuen Wan MTR station (exit A2), take bus No 66M to Tuen Mun. To the right of the road the vista is dominated by mountains, while to the left is a good view of the ★ **Tsing Ma Bridge** ⓼. Tuen Mun is one of the territory's oldest settlements. During the Tang Dynasty (618–907), a fortress guarded the entrance to the Pearl River. From the 11th century, the Tang clan from the province

Star Attraction
● **Sam Tung Uk Museum**

Below: Sam Tung Uk Museum exhibit
Bottom: paper figures at Sam Tung Uk Museum

Map on page 66

of Jiangxi settled in the region and farmed the fertile hinterland. Today, Tuen Mun is another of the huge so-called New Towns.

Disembark at Tai Hing Estate terminus, turn right along Tai Fong Street and left onto the Tsun Wen Road. Beyond the highway bridge is the ★★ **Ching Chung Koon Monastery** **77**. Also known as the Temple of the Evergreen Pine Trees, it was founded by a Taoist association in 1949. The temple is known for its collection of 4,000 books on Taoism and Chinese history, and for its more than 1,000 bonsai trees.

Leave the monastery by the path to the left of the entrance. You'll see the Ching Chung Light Rail Transit (LRT) stop ahead. Cross the tracks and take the No 615 towards Yuen Long to the Ping Shan stop.

Almost free lunch

A large part of the Ching Chung Koon Monastery complex serves as a home for the aged run by the social organisation of the Taoist Association, which also serves visitors a vegetarian meal at midday for a nominal sum.

PING SHAN HERITAGE TRAIL

You may want to skip Tuen Mun altogether and take the No 68M bus directly from Tsuen Wan to Ping Shan. Enjoy the views of Tsing Ma Bridge to the left, and disembark at Castle Peak Road in about 25 minutes. From here, catch the No 610, 614 or 615 LRT to Ping Shan. (From near Tin Hau MTR, bus No 968 runs one hour to Yuen Long.)

Walk back a little from the station and then turn right into Ping Ha Road. After approximately 400yds (about 370m) you will reach the Hung Shing Temple, the starting point for the ★★ **Ping Shan Heritage Trail** **78**.

Novices at Ching Chung Koon Monastery

The footpath, about ½ mile (1 km) long, is clearly signposted and leads through the villages of Ping Shan past small temples and ancestral halls to Hong Kong's only remaining pagoda. Villagers allow visitors to look round most of the monuments on the trail between 9am and 5pm (closed from 1–2pm for lunch, Tuesday and public holidays), but please respect the fact that they are private monuments.

Visitors with a bent for heritage and culture will appreciate this tour the most, as the area quite remote. The trail is well-signposted, and takes an hour or more to explore.

HUNG SHING TEMPLE

The **Hung Shing Temple** is a simple building originally built in 1767 and rebuilt in 1866, and dedicated to an exceptional Tang Dynasty official. Skilled in astronomy, he provided fishermen with accurate weather forecasts – a talent much valued by simple fisherfolk.

Down an alley to the right lie the **Kun Ting Study Hall** (1870) and **Ching Shu Hin**, which functioned as a school and guesthouse, respectively, for the Tang family. Both are currently closed to the public but can be appreciated from the outside.

Star Attractions
● **Ching Chung Koon Monastery**
● **Ping Shan Heritage Trail**

Below: Hung Shing temple deity
Bottom: Tang Ancestral Hall funeral tablets

TANG ANCESTRAL HALL

On the edge of the village lies the main **Tang Ancestral Hall**, one of which has existed on this site for some 700 years, according to clan records. The **Yu Kiu Ancestral Hall** (also closed to the public) immediately to the south dates from the early 16th century. Both buildings consist of three halls connected by two internal courtyards, used for ancestor worship and also as a venue for family meetings and celebrations.

Wooden ancestral tablets, called 'soul tablets', of entire generations or of individual family members are displayed inside the ancestral hall. These provide a unique record of Chinese culture, as

Map
on page
66

many of these artefacts were destroyed in mainland China during the Cultural Revolution, when village elders were forced to tear down ancestral halls and torch the revered soul tablets.

WALLED VILLAGE AND A PAGODA

*Altar and (below) pagoda
at Tsui Shing Lau*

Further along the trail stands the walled village of **Sheung Cheung Wai** ❼. Only a few remnants of the old village still exist, as new houses have been built within the walls and old ones converted, but this is very much a living village. Outside the fortification, a traditional **Altar to the Earth God** has been restored. It is a small platform on which a stone represents the earth deity.

The last monument on the trail is the hexagonal **Tsui Shing Lau Pagoda**, dating from the 14th or 15th century. It is 42ft (13m) tall with three storeys, each bearing a name related to the stars. Built to ward off bad *fung shui* influences, it originally nestled between woods and a small lake. Today, the concrete backdrop of Tin Shui Wai's housing estates makes viewing it from a distance before moving on not such a bad idea.

Beyond the walled village, follow the footpath to the left across the reservoir and up to the road. Cross to the other side to take the LRT No 610, 614 or 615 back to Yuen Long, from where bus No 968 returns to Hong Kong Island.

TAI FU TAI

Taking a taxi is the easiest way to reach **San Tin village**, situated between Yuen Long and Sheung Shui. The main attraction is the ★★ **Tai Fu Tai** ❽ (daily 9am–1pm and 2pm–5pm; closed Tuesday and public holidays) in Wing Ping Tsuen hamlet. This gracious residence with three courtyards was built in 1865 for Man Cheung-luen, an official whom the Qing Dynasty emperor honoured with the title *tai fu* or 'mandarin'.

The owner's portrait hangs above the altar opposite the entrance, flanked by pictures of his first wife and his eldest son on the right and his second wife and third son on the left. Two plaques record compliments received by Man Cheung-luen from the imperial court on passing the civil service entrance examination. In accordance with regulations passed by the Qing Dynasty, which ruled China until 1911, the inscriptions, are written in both Manchurian and Chinese.

The living quarters lead off from a central courtyard, as do the bedrooms on the first floor. Servants lived in a side wing. On the way to the kitchen quarters on the right side is a hollow tree trunk which was used for pressing groundnuts.

SEVEN SONS

Apart from the main fireplace in the kitchen there are seven smaller ones. According to legend, Man Cheung-luen had seven sons, all of whom married and continued to live in the house with their respective wives. Because the women were unable to agree on domestic arrangements, each was entitled to her own fireplace.

A 10-minute walk past Tai Fu Tai brings you to Fan Tin Tsuen hamlet and the **Man Lun Fung Ancestral Hall**, where the Mans have venerated their ancestors since the 17th century.

The quickest way back to Kowloon or Central from San Tin is to take a No 76K bus or taxi to Sheung Shui KCR station and proceed by train as far as the MTR interchange at Kowloon Tong.

Star Attraction
● **Tai Fu Tai**

Heritage tour
Since Tai Fu Tai is extremely difficult to reach by public transportation, join the HKTB-sponsored half-day Heritage Tour (tel: 2368 7112), which operates four times weekly and combines insightful interpretation of several historical and cultural sights with convenient coach transportation. The tour takes in Man Mo Temple in Tai Po, the unique Lam Tsuen Wishing Tree, Tang Chung Ling Ancestral Hall and Lo Wai Walled Village before culminating with a visit to the stately residence of Tai Fu Tai. Time permitting, the driver may swing by the border on your return, allowing you a glimpse of Shenzhen.

Doorway, Tai Fu Tai Residence

Map
below

Excursion 1: Lantau Island

Mui Wo – Cheung Sha Upper Beach – Tai O – Po Lin Monastery – Big Buddha – Lantau Peak – Tung Chung

Almost twice the size of Hong Kong, **Lantau** was once an island of tranquility, spiritual retreats and small fishing communities. Today, the Hong Kong International Airport is in Chek Lap Kok on the northwest coast, the population stands at almost 50,000, a New Town has engulfed the sleepy coastal village of Tung Chung, and reclamation works are underway for a Hong Kong Disneyland which opens in 2005. Yet much of the island remains rural – for now – making a day trip to the fishing village of Tai O and Po Lin Monastery a welcome respite from life in the big city.

Ferry to Lantau Island

MUI WO

To reach Lantau, catch a ferry (tel: 2131 8181) from **Outlying Islands Ferry Pier** to **Mui Wo**, whose English name is **Silvermine Bay**, although

the eponymous mine is long gone. The village itself is unremarkable; board the No 1 bus waiting at the bus station in front of the pier. It takes 40 minutes to reach Tai O on the other end of the island. Just out of Silvermine Bay, the road starts to climb the first hills, typical of the landscape on the island. On the way to Pui O, it passes the start of several hiking trails in **North Lantau Country Park**, many of them leading towards **Sunset Peak**, at 2,781ft (869m), the second-highest mountain on Lantau.

CHEUNG SHA UPPER BEACH

Numerous picnic and grill areas border the road. **Pui O** is a small village with large numbers of holiday apartments provided by Hong Kong firms for their employees' use during weekends and short annual vacations. The little beach is not particularly attractive. From here the road leads off to **Chi Ma Wan Peninsula**, where, in rough countryside, archaeologists have found lime kilns and relics from the Bronze Age.

Visitors intending to include a beach interlude in their itinerary should stop off at the 2-mile (3-km) ★★ **Cheung Sha Upper Beach** – Hong Kong's largest, with fairly clean water. The beach is relatively empty except on hot summer weekends. Changing rooms and showers are available. There are a few local seafood restaurants on the beach, but those in the know head for **The Stoep** (tel: 2980 2699) for excellent South African fare and perfectly chilled beers.

The government takes advantage of the remoteness of Lantau to keep crime under control. On the slope behind Tong Fuk are several prisons and reform centres for drug addicts, and there is another in Tung Wan, below Shek Pik reservoir. The bus route crosses the 173-ft (54-m) dam. Drinking water is pumped through a pipeline to Hong Kong Island. From the reservoir visitors will get their first glimpse of the big Buddha statue at Po Lin Monastery.

Beyond the reservoir the bus slows considerably as the road climbs steep switchbacks, giving

Star Attraction
● Cheung Sha Upper Beach

Discovery Bay
Though of little interest to tourists, Discovery Bay is a unique housing development in northern Lantau that includes both a golf course and tennis courts. One of the nicest places for families to settle in Hong Kong, 'Disco Bay' has its own rapid ferry system to and from Central.

Cheung Sha Beach scene

Map on page 82

passengers plenty of time to study the surrounding mountains. After crossing the pass, the road runs downhill into the fertile Tai O plain. On the slopes are perched several splendid little monasteries with fine views across the lowlands.

TAI O

During the last century, what is now the sleepy fishing village of ★ **Tai O** was of great importance for the island. Its location on the north coast of Lantau overlooks the Pearl River Estuary. Further upriver lies Guangzhou, which as the city of Canton was the most important trading and economic centre in South China. It had its own viceroy and was also the only port at which foreign traders were permitted to disembark.

The population of Tai O, by contrast, was primarily employed in fishing and the salt industry, two important and profitable economic spheres at the time. They still play a part in the economy today, although rice farming, duck raising and the manufacture of shrimp paste provide a broader basis, a fact which can be sniffed as you cross the village.

Tai O is still a fascinating village built on stilts although its character is changing now as modern apartment blocks gradually replace the old wooden structures.

From the end of the car park where the buses stop, turn right into the main street, along which every third shop seems to sell dried or pickled fish.

Parallel to the main road, a creek separates the main island from the little offshore island of Fu Shan. Until 1996, the channel was traversed by a flat punt which was pulled backwards and forwards by two elderly women. This has been replaced by a Chinese pagoda-style drawbridge, which provides a good view of the settlement of rather ramshackle, metal-sheeted **stilt houses** rising out of the mud.

For some, this kind of dwelling represents the best alternative to living on a boat, but the government apparently thinks differently and has slated these traditional houses for demolition.

Shop-cum-home

In the traditional houses of Tai O, there are no clearly defined boundaries between shop and house; the family may be sitting at the back and eating, or the children perched on a wooden bench in front of the television set. At night, some family members will retire to the first floor to sleep, whilst others put up their camp beds in the shop. Many of the doors are still adorned with traditional posters of watchmen, or have guardian figures painted directly onto the doors.

Stilt houses at Tai O

New accommodation has already been built, but many – particularly the older residents – are extremely reluctant to leave.

TWO TEMPLES

It's worth walking past the stilt houses to the ★ **Hau Wong Temple** built on a narrow spit of land surrounded by water. Dating from 1699, this is the oldest of four temples in the territory dedicated to Yang Liang-je, an uncle of the last two Song dynasty emperors, who as boys sought refuge from the Mongols on Lantau when the latter invaded the empire at the end of the 13th century. Look carefully and you might see huge whale bones and swordfish beaks stacked inside.

Head back towards the market place at the heart of the village. In the market square lies **Kwan Tai Temple**, dedicated to the god of war and justice. Within the triple-winged building, whose interior is black with smoke, are a number of wooden figures and simple stones before which the faithful offer incense sticks or fruit.

PO LIN MONASTERY

From Tai O, the next destination should be the ★★ **Po Lin Monastery**, situated at Ngong Ping in the glorious upland scenery of central Lantau. The

Star Attraction
● Po Lin Monastery

Below: Hau Wong Temple
Bottom: Tai O's fishing boats

Map
on page
82

cheapest way to get there is by bus: the No 21 leaves every hour for Ngong Ping on the hour between 11am and 3pm from Tai O bus stop. Taxis can also usually be found waiting here.

The first monks settled on the high plateau of Ngong Ping in 1905. When their numbers increased following the founding of the Chinese Republic in 1912, the Po Lin Monastery was officially dedicated in 1927. Until the 1970s it was an almost unknown and remote complex, but nowadays the monks and nuns have mastered the art of temple tourism quite well.

It used to be possible to stay overnight at the monastery until the government discovered that the enterprising brethren had no licence to conduct such business. All that remains of their hospitality is the Chinese vegetarian lunch which can be eaten in the refectory following the purchase of computerised place-allocation tickets.

Below and bottom: different vistas of Po Lin Monastery

TEMPLE LAYOUT

The temple area of the monastery follows the traditional plan and architecture of Chinese Buddhist temples. All the important buildings lie one behind the other on a single axis. Their conspicuous roofs have upturned eaves, and the principal ones stand on high platforms. In the first hall, visitors are greeted by the portly, laughing fig-

ure of Milefo. He represents the 10th-century monk Qi Ci, who at his death revealed himself to be an incarnation of Maitreya, the Buddha of the Future. He is surrounded by four heavenly guardians, one for each point of the compass. Behind him stands Weito, messenger to the gods.

Between the entrance hall and the main temple pavilion is a line of large bronze vessels for incense sticks. Two tablets symbolising the Wheel of Life flank the entrance staircase. In the main pavilion, three gilt Buddha statues adorn the altar: in the middle is Sakyamuni, the historical Buddha, to the left, the Buddha of the Past and to the right, the Healing Buddha. Prayer flags hang from the roof, and carved wooden frames support the drum and bell, both symbols of time.

THE BIG BUDDHA

The rooms at the rear serve the monks and nuns for private meditation and study. Occasionally, visitors are allowed a glimpse of a very small and extremely valuable Burmese Buddha statue made of white jade.

At the other end of the scale is the huge **bronze Buddha** opposite the temple, weighing in at 202 tonnes and claimed to be the world's largest outdoor seated Buddha. Planning began in 1974, but a succession of problems held up production and the official dedication ceremony was not held until 29 December 1993. A staircase of 268 steps leads up to the statue, symbolising the merit Buddhists must earn in this life in preparation for the next. At the top is the **Tian Tan**, the 'Altar of Heaven', on which the Buddha sits on a bed of lotus. In the Buddhist religion the lotus symbolises purity, for it grows in muddy pools and still brings forth pure flowers.

Inside the altar is a valuable wooden statue of the Bodhisattva Khsitigarbha made of very hard *nanmu* wood. A bronze bell weighing 6 tonnes and engraved with Buddhist inscriptions is rung 108 times every morning, with a computer to control the 'lucky' number of chimes. There are oil paintings depicting the life of the Buddha. It is

> **Big crowds**
> Though the bronze Buddha is an impressive sight, be prepared to share the experience with plenty of others. The big Buddha at Po Lin Monastery is the top site for tourists to Lantau. Arrive early and you may beat the crowds.

Po Lin Monastery's Buddha statue occupies prime position

Map
on page
82

also believed that relics of the Buddha are preserved here. Bearing in mind that the Buddha was cremated soon after his death and that a number of temples also claim to own relics, a certain amount of scepticism may be called for.

LANTAU PEAK

A footpath leads off from the roundabout past Hong Kong's only **tea plantation** before climbing steeply to the top of Hong Kong's second tallest mountain, ★ **Lantau Peak** (3,064ft/934m), for spectacular panoramic views.

From here, it is possible to continue along a steep trail to the summit of Sunset Peak, and then descend into Tung Chung, another New Town. However, an approach from the other direction is easier on the knees – Tung Chung to Sunset Peak and then Lantau Peak. Allow at least five hours.

Take a hike
Lantau offers plenty of hiking trails, including the 70-kilometre Lantau Trail. All it takes to get started is a decent map, solid walking shoes, drinking water, sunscreen and a hat. Country park maps are available from the Government Publications Centre in Queensway, Admiralty.

TUNG CHUNG

Hiking trail at Lantau Island

You can also reach **Tung Chung** in under 50 minutes by the No 23 bus (10 and 40 minutes past the hour until 5.10pm; 6.10pm and 7.10pm; more frequent on Sunday and public holidays). There is also a concrete footpath providing you have the energy, and at least 1½ hours to spare.

From here, Kowloon or Hong Kong Island are 30 minutes away by MTR, but you could linger a while to visit the early 19th-century Chinese ★ **Tung Chung Fort** (information centre open 9am–4pm except Tuesday and public holidays). Constructed in 1832, this was the base from which the Chinese army controlled coastal shipping until the British leased Lantau in 1898. At the end of the 1930s the local residents used the fort as a school, until the Japanese forces arrived. There is an exhibition room in which a display of photographs documents the history of the complex.

Notice the almost surreal juxtaposition of Tung Chung 'old town', with its traditional stilt houses and picturesque ★ **Hau Wong Temple**, against the backdrop of **Hong Kong International Airport** at Chek Lap Kok.

Excursion 2: Cheung Chau

Pak Tai Temple – Cheung Chau Bun Festival – Tung Wan and Kwun Yam Wan beaches – Cheung Po Tsai cave

During the week, life on the smaller islands in the shadow of Lantau continues at a gentle and unhurried pace. Come weekends, however, the ferries disgorge hordes of day trippers who flock to the beaches and occupy the little weekend guest rooms. So, if at all possible, pick a quiet weekday for your visit.

It will take you around two to three hours to complete a gentle stroll around the temple and market village of **Cheung Chau**, famous for its annual Bun Festival in May, when throngs of visitors make their way across to the tiny, dumbbell-shaped island steeped in old tradition. You will also find an abundance of tasty and fresh seafood, stunning views out across the sea and gentle island ways.

Below: Cheung Chau's resident fixtures
Bottom: the Cheung Chau waterfront

PAK TAI TEMPLE

The outing to Cheung Chau Island begins on the ferry service (tel: 2131 8181) leaving the **Outlying Islands Ferry Pier** in Central. A fast ferry should take about 40 minutes.

Below: Cheung Chau's Praya waterfront

The quay at Cheung Chau, meaning 'Long Island', juts out from the bustling waterfront promenade. Head left along the **Praya** (harbour promenade), and you will soon reach the first restaurants on **Pak She Praya Road**, and then a sports ground, behind which stands ★★**Pak Tai Temple**, which dates from 1783. The temple is less than a 10-minute walk from the ferry.

RULER OF THE NORTH

Pak Tai is the Cantonese name for the Ruler of the North. According to legend, he received from the Jade Emperor, the highest Taoist deity, command over 12 heavenly legions in order to fight the King of Demons, who had among his forces a grey tortoise and a giant snake. Of course, Pak Tai was victorious over the forces of evil. He is usually represented in a sitting position, with his feet resting on a tortoise and a snake.

In 1777, when the plague had broken out on Cheung Chau, the islanders brought over the local Pak Tai statue from their native village on the mainland (according to one version of the legend, local fishermen found the statue floating in the sea). But whatever the version, the island was spared further visitations by the pestilence from this time onwards, so a temple was built out of gratitude for the divine intervention that drove away the evil spirits. The statue is flanked by the dark figures of Thousand-Li-Eye and Good-Wind-Ear, two popular figures from Chinese mythology who are famous for their remarkable sensory powers. The dynamic duo are reputedly able to see and hear all, from any distance.

CHEUNG CHAU BUN FESTIVAL

Each year in May, the colourful ★★ **Cheung Chau Bun Festival** is held in front of the temple. The ritual was apparently initiated when human bones were discovered during temple construction. Fearing that the temple would be haunted by the spirits which

had been disturbed, the island's inhabitants sought to appease them by putting out offerings of steamed buns. Today, the event is celebrated by the erection of three 52-ft (16-m) bamboo towers, each piled with some 5,000 pink and white lotus-paste buns.

Religious groups set up stands in which deities and temple paintings are displayed for the duration of the festival. The festival lasts for about eight or nine days, and for three of them the islanders turn strict vegetarians.

Chinese opera, lion dances and musical performances take place on the square. Statues from all the wayside and village temples on the island are carried to Pak Tai Temple, and ferries to and from the island are jam-packed with visitors.

FLOATING CHILDREN

The highlight of the festival is undoubtedly the **grand procession** in which the statues are returned to their homes accompanied by a brightly-coloured procession of floats, banners and dragon dances. The key characters in the procession are always portrayed by children, who wear colourful, traditional costumes. More spectacularly, they are borne along the route as they perch on concealed poles so that they seem to 'float' high above the crowd. Amazingly, whether

Star Attractions
● **Pak Tai Temple**
● **Cheung Chau Bun Festival**

Pick a date
It's always difficult to ascertain the actual date of the Bun Festival, which is loosely based on the lunar calendar. This is because the island's committee must first 'confer' with the deity Pak Tai less than a month before the celebrations to determine an auspicious date.

In 2002, for instance, the committee agreed to hold the grand procession on 19 May, a Sunday (and therefore a holiday). There was talk of fixing the date on the birthdate of Buddha – an official public holiday – but it is unclear whether this will be implemented. To be sure, check with the HKTB (tel: 2508 1234).

Lotus buns feature prominently in the Bun Festival

Map on page 90

Below: Altar to the Earth Deity
Bottom: testing the waters at Tung Wan

kneeling or standing they remain, like dolls, absolutely still, well above the heads of the spectators and making quite a spectacle.

Until recently, it was a ritual for young men to climb the towers the morning after and pick as many buns as possible. The one who accumulated the most buns from the highest points on the tower would enjoy the greatest fortune during the following year. The inherent dangers of the climb, however, forced the practice to be abandoned; a collapsed tower in 1978 resulted in more than just smashed buns.

Sadly, for those who don't like to see the old ways disappear, the buns are now collected in a more orderly manner and distributed among the island's inhabitants.

WINDSURFERS' BEACHES

From the temple, walk down Pak She Street to the intersection with Kwok Man Road. At the crossroads is a small **Altar to the Earth Deity** which is always adorned with incense sticks and offerings. In former times, these simple animist shrines in which the earth deity is represented only by a stone, could be seen in virtually every district. They bear witness to the wide variety of Chinese religious beliefs and the differing levels of abstraction involved.

Diagonally opposite is San Hing Street, which is lined with typical village shops and leads straight into the alleys of the bustling **market quarter**. Here you will find traditional village hats, Chinese medicines, dried foodstuffs and joss sticks on sale alongside modern household goods.

At the end, turn left along Tung Wun Road to the sandy beaches of **Tung Wan** and **Kwun Yam Wan**. The bay is very popular with windsurfers, and the **Cheung Chau Windsurfing Centre and Café** (tel: 2981 8316), which is owned by the uncle of Hong Kong windsurfing champion and 1996 Olympic gold medallist Lee Lai-shan ('San-san') sometimes provides lessons, in addition to equipment rentals.

The centre is at the south end of the bay, past the modern **Warwick Hotel** (tel: 2981 0081), something of an eyesore. This is Cheung Chau's poshest hotel and if you feel like treating yourself it is a possible choice for an overnight stay. You may get a room without booking during the week (HK$490), but do make reservations ahead of time for weekend visits (HK$690).

> **Tightly knit**
> Despite its relatively small size, the towns of Cheung Chau are rather densely packed, predominantly with Chinese immigrants. The population in 2001 soared to 23,300.

ISLAND STROLL

The path below the hotel passes a 3,000-year-old geometric rock carving, rediscovered in 1970. If you want a longer walk around the southern part of the island, follow Kwun Yam Wan Road up the hill behind the hotel to Peak Road. Head south and follow Peak Road until you come to a cemetery and then a path down to **Pak Tso Wan Beach**.

Further around the promontory is the **Cheung Po Tsai Cave**, where the eponymous Qing Dynasty pirate allegedly settled with his band after receiving amnesty, about 30 years before the British arrived; and an old Tin Hau Temple.

Return to the ferry pier by *sampan* from **Sai Wan village** – there are plenty of *sampan*, also known as *kaido*, to choose from – or continue round the coast on the wide road that leads back to the waterfront. Turn right just before you reach the covered market for dinner at **Lotus Thai** (tel: 2891 2432), or head back to one of the seafood restaurants on the Praya.

Sizing up a fresh catch

Map on page 95

Excursion 3: Lamma

Yung Shue Wan – Hung Shing Ye Beach – Lo So Shing Beach – Sok Kwu Wan

Lamma Island (population 5,550), the third largest island in the territory after Lantau and Hong Kong, has a reputation for great seafood restaurants and the 'alternative' lifestyle of some of its expatriate community. This walk gives you a taste of both. As with Cheung Chau, Lamma Island is a sleepy hamlet during the week but erupts with boatloads of day trippers on weekends and public holidays, so try to go on a weekday.

The gently rolling, north-to-south walk between ferry piers takes a couple hours, but it is easy to wander at an even more leisurely pace through the eclectic handicraft shops, or to raise a pint or three to the good life in this charming little enclave, free of both cars and high-rises.

YUNG SHUE WAN

The ferry trip (tel: 2815 6063) from the **Outlying Islands Ferry Pier** in Central takes half an hour. Once on the island, follow the crowds along **Yung Shue Wan Main Street** round the newly reclaimed patch of land (formerly the harbour) scheduled for further development and past the

All fired up
Despite the fact that firecrackers are prohibited under Hong Kong law, outlying islands such as Lamma regularly flout such regulations. At any rate, Lamma's minimal police force, who can be seen zipping around the island on mountain bikes, is powerless to fight the traditions. To ring in the Lunar New Year in style – and more traditionally, to scare away the evil spirits of the previous year – the deafening roar of firecrackers echoes from midnight till dawn on this day through the narrow, concreted alleyways of Yung Shue Wan and other villages of the Outlying Islands.

Main street, Yung Shue Wan

open-air Chinese restaurants, grocery shops, gift shops and cafés serving Western food.

Laid back **Deli Lamma** (tel: 2982 1583), Indian nosh at **Toochka** (tel: 2982 0159) or traditional *dim sum* at the **Sampan** restaurant (tel: 2982 2388) are good bets for a late breakfast or light lunch. There is a well-tended **Tin Hau Temple** behind the sports field past the Bookworm Café; the goddess' birthday is celebrated here each May.

Star Attraction
● Lamma's seafood restaurants

Inside the Tin Hau Temple

BEACHES

After strolling through the village, you should follow signposts indicating a turn left to **Hung Shing Ye**. As the three-storey modern tiled houses gradually peter out, the path winds past small vegetable plots and dotted hamlets, with the three chimneys of Lamma Power Station looming ever-present on your right. **Hung Shing Ye Beach** is relatively clean, with changing rooms, snack stalls and a small café.

At the far end of the beach the narrow concrete path starts to climb more steeply, towards a hill with an observation pavilion. Many day trippers turn back at this halfway point – all the more reason for you to carry on.

The path descends into **Lo So Shing**, a sleepy hamlet of traditional Chinese houses. Enjoy a wander through the narrow alleyways between these lovely old homes. Either follow the signs to the pretty (and relatively secluded) ★ **Lo So Shing Beach** or continue directly to **Sok Kwu Wan** (Picnic Bay).

The north side of the bay, once quarried, has recently been planted and landscaped in anticipation of future development. The bay itself is used for intensive fish farming, with much of the produce going to the ★★ **seafood restaurants** on the waterfront that make Lamma a popular destination for local residents on weekends.

There are ferries back to Central every two hours or so; or you can ask the restaurant staff about taking a *kaido* or *sampan* to Aberdeen.

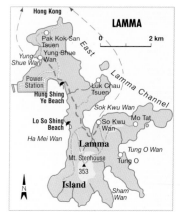

Religion and Superstition

Hong Kong may be one of the world's most modern and technologically advanced cities, boasting innovative building design and every convenience, but it is culturally still very Chinese. You see it everywhere: in the calligraphy of the street and shop signs, the residents practising *tai chi* in the parks and playing *mahjong*, and in the temples and shrines everywhere.

East Asian beliefs rest on the twin pillars of Confucianism, which covers all public matters, and Taoism, which provides the individual creed. These two philosophies permeate everyday life although they are radically opposed and create conflict in day-to-day behaviour, which individuals must seek to resolve. Together, they form the basis for traditional family celebrations, public festivals and a wide range of symbolic acts.

> **A private affair**
> Unlike Christianity, Confucianism and Taoism have no church, and therefore no institution to govern, regulate and dogmatise faith. Religion is a private affair with which everyone must come to terms alone. However, the religious aspect is only one small element in the wide-ranging philosophies of the East and has very little to do with original thoughts. Instead, it is surrounded by a network of legends and myths, with simple ceremonies and colourful spectacles to guarantee universal appeal.

CONFUCIANISM

Confucius (551–479BC) was the son of a minor nobleman in what is today the province of Shandong. He lived in unruly times, and wanted to become an advisor to a princely court in order to present to the ruler his thoughts on peace and order. In doing so he referred to the 'ideal rulers' Yao and Shun, whose only disadvantage was that their origins lay in the world of mythology.

The state declared the theories of Confucius to be largely idealistic. Confucius saw the 'ideal' society as consisting of a strict hierarchy in which rulers had the power to make decisions for ministers, fathers for sons, husbands for wives and older brothers for younger ones. Only relationships between friends were regarded as equal. In return, the rulers were required to treat their subjects with benevolence and to care for them.

Left and below: Po Fook Ancestor Hall

AN IMPERIAL LEGACY

The 'school' of Confucius had virtually no influence during his lifetime and the Master was denied a high position and had to eke out an existence as a wandering tutor. His pupils, however, achieved considerable influence and, in their position as princely advisors, developed the theory of the 'mandate of Heaven', which was to legitimise the ruler's claim to power.

During the Han Dynasty (206BC–220AD), the emperor was so convinced by the doctrines of Confucius that he added paragraphs concerning the maintenance of power and declared them to be the national doctrine. The effects can still be observed in some East Asian countries where societies are characterised by lack of social mobility, and authoritarian regimes govern the political scene.

Below: praying with incense sticks
Bottom: ancestral tablets

FILIAL PIETY

Strong family ties emanate from the respect due to one's ancestors, a duty instilled into the eldest son. It is believed that the soul leaves the body at death but finds no rest for three generations, haunting and influencing the lives of those left behind. In order to ensure that the soul is contented it must be given those things which it needed during its earthly life.

On special days set aside for paying tribute to one's ancestors, fake paper money is burned on the grave or in the temple, borne by smoke into the spirit world. Similarly, most Chinese homes are adorned with altars for burning incense and

remembering ancestors. The souls thus acquire god-like status: they are revered but not worshipped in the true sense of the word. Neither the souls of the departed nor the gods are seen as capable of human action, and the tablets devoted to ancestors or divinities are seen as memorials or means of concentration.

TAOISM

This belief provides the link to Taoism, which concentrates exclusively on the individual and his ability to find his individual *Tao*, or 'way' – in other words, an attitude which is at one with his nature. The Taoist often finds this in the behaviour pattern known as the *wu wei*, which is frequently translated as 'inaction', or rather, the absence of unnatural, forced or aggressive action. Such non-interference should not be viewed as passivity but rather that which involves activity in harmony with nature.

The 'tao' of art
The influence of Taoism in art cannot be overestimated. Painters, calligraphers and poets were limited by clearly laid-down traditions regarding technique and subject, but in the execution of their art and their attitude to life they devoted themselves to Taoism. The oft-repeated scenes depicted in typical landscape paintings reveal Taoist thoughts. Vast precipitous mountains swathed in clouds dominate the picture, while human figures insignificant. Nature is the all-powerful element in which man should seek his place without contradiction as far as this is possible.

LAO TZU

The development of Taoism is ascribed to the hermit Lao Tzu (circa 6th century BC), although there is evidence that the *Tao Te Ching* ('The Way and the Virtue') is a later collection of aphorisms. Closely linked to Taoism is the idea of *yin* and *yang*, two opposing forces which each bear the essence of the other within them and which find balance in a perfect synthesis.

The *yang* stands for masculinity, strength, hardness, brightness, heat, activity and the south; the *yin* is the symbol of femininity, weakness, softness, darkness, cold, passivity and the north. Thus is the natural way of the universe reflected in the ebb and flow of human life.

POPULAR BELIEFS

Taoism, like Confucianism, was originally not a religion. It developed its popular forms only after the arrival of Buddhism in China, circa 65AD. The Buddhism that is prevalent in China

Performing tai chi excercises

today is Mahayana Buddhism, or the Way of the Greater Vehicle. This doctrine proclaims that deliverance and entry into nirvana as a release from all earthly suffering can also be achieved with the assistance of the *bodhisattva*. These are Buddhist saints who postpone their own enlightenment in order to help others. The best-known *bodhisattva* is Avalokiteshvara, who underwent a gender transformation in China to become Guanyin (Kwun Yum in Cantonese), the much-loved Goddess of Mercy.

TAOIST DEITIES

Taoism also acquired a vast pantheon of gods. Pride of place is occupied by the Jade Emperor, followed by divinities of lesser importance. The second level is occupied by the Eight Immortals, originally historic personages of the 7th–10th century about whom legends grew. Like the *bodhisattva*, they can return to earth to help mankind.

The seven men and one woman each possess a characteristic sign by which they can be recognised and which can frequently be spotted adorning the poles in the temples of Hong Kong: a fly-swatter, a gourd, a basket of flowers, etc. A vast number of highly revered earthly beings – originally poets, doctors, officials and generals – occupy the third level. Hong Kong's best-loved Taoist divinity is Tin Hau (which accounts for the large number of Tin Hau temples in Hong Kong), the patroness of fishermen and sailors.

FUNG SHUI

The Taoist philosophy of nature also gave rise to the geomancy known in Cantonese as *fung shui* (in Mandarin, *feng shui*), literally translated as 'wind-water'. *Fung shui* asserts that buildings should also harmonise with their surroundings, that they should be protected and should have no sharp corners. The most favourable location for a building is with a mountain behind, if possible to the north. The south and the front side of the building should open onto a plain. The explanation is simple and

> **Flexible 'fung shui'**
> In the mythical matters of *fung shui*, the Chinese have become masters of pragmatism. A dragon supposedly lives in every mountain, but the most favourable building locations are constantly compromised by the shortage of land. Therefore, minor constructional additions, like a strategically placed mirror, fountain or stone lion, can divert bad currents.

A Repulse Bay condo with a hole to allow bad 'fung shui' to pass through

practical: the ideas arose in north China, where icy winds blew from the north, so that it made sense to shelter beneath a mountain. Apart from determining the location of buildings, *fung shui* is also used to position the graves of ancestors, since their influence on the living is crucial.

NUMEROLOGY

In many societies, the number 8 is a lucky number, because it can be repeated an infinite number of times without removing the pen from the paper. In China, too, the number 8 symbolises infinity and eternal life. It is thus no coincidence that the Tao immortals are eight in number. In Hong Kong, moreover, the Cantonese names for several numbers sound similar to words with completely different meanings. Thus, the word for 'one' is associated with the word for 'must', 'two' is linked to 'easy' or 'light' and the word for 'eight' to 'excess'.

Conversely, the number four is a bad omen: the Cantonese word sounds like that for 'death'. People have made up an infinite variety of ways to support this superstition; for example, Hong Kong citizens may make sure that their car registration plates consist only of 'good' numbers. Number 28 could be taken to mean 'win excess easily'; even better is a quadrupling of the number of

Below: the Chinese consider gold fish as lucky
Bottom: Tin Hau Temple deity

excess: '8888'. Most prestigious of all, however, are one-digit numbers.

Number combinations containing the number '4', on the other hand, are avoided. Worst of all is '14', for it means 'must die'. For this reason, many buildings have no 14th floor as no one would want to live on this level. Sometimes, the number '13' is also missing in order to appease Western superstitions. The most auspicious day of this century was, of course, 8.8.88, a day on which the registry offices had to put in overtime performing marriage ceremonies, and countless new businesses were founded.

Festivals and Events

Traditional festivals are a natural product of religious and superstitious beliefs and mostly honour individual gods or ancestors. They follow the cycle of the Chinese lunar calendar, which begins with the Lunar New Year festival on the first full moon between mid-January and mid-February.

LUNAR NEW YEAR

When the **Lunar New Year** comes, families spring-clean their homes, buy new furnishings or possessions, redecorate – especially with 'lucky' pictures of fish, because the words 'luck' and

Below: lion dance at a Lunar New Year parade
Bottom: fireworks explode over the HK skyline

'fish', are near homonyms. Above all, the ancestral altar must be cleaned, as according to legend, the Kitchen God ascends to heaven on the eve of the New Year to give the Jade Emperor a report on the family. In order to ensure that he tells only the sweetest stories, some Chinese smear the mouth of his image with honey.

According to Confucian tradition, superiors must show their subordinates their goodwill at the Lunar New Year. On this day, this usually involves giving *lai see*, or gifts of 'lucky' money in little red envelopes, red being the colour of good fortune. Children, unmarried relatives and junior workers will be remembered on this occasion. People wish each other *kung hei fat choi*, or much prosperity and success in the new lunar year.

The festival itself, however, is spent at home feasting and celebrating with the family. Many take the opportunity to visit relatives across the border; and the city, which for the rest of the year does not seem to sleep, grinds to a veritable halt for several days.

Officially, New Year festivities end on the 15th day with the **Spring Lantern Festival** (Yuen Siu), the Chinese equivalent of Valentine's Day.

OTHER CHINESE FESTIVALS

In April is the **Ching Ming Festival**, when thousands of people visit the cemeteries to pay respect to their ancestors by cleaning the graves, lighting incense and offering gifts.

Although the **Tin Hau Festival** celebrating the goddess' birthday on the 23rd day of the third lunar month (April/May) is not an official holiday, it is marked by numerous processions in which the statues of the goddess are carried through the streets or, more appropriately, paraded ceremoniously through the harbour by boat.

The **Cheung Chau Bun Festival** is celebrated every May with processions, dragon dances, etc., when the spirits of those whose bones were disturbed during the construction of the Pak Tai Temple are appeased with offerings of steamed buns *(see pages 90–91 for more details)*.

> **Official fireworks**
> In the past, local Hong Kong residents arranged vast firework displays at the start of the Lunar New Year to chase away evil spirits. But today, private firework displays are banned on safety grounds. By way of compensation, the government sends a few millions' worth of fireworks rocketing into the air above the harbour every year.

Cheung Chau Bun Festival Parade

Art house film fare

Hong Kong cinemas regularly feature the latest Hollywood blockbusters (English with Chinese subtitles) and locally-produced action movies (usually in Chinese with English subtitles). For art-house movies, try the Hong Kong Arts Centre or Cine-Art House, both in Wanchai, or Broadway Cinematheque in Yau Ma Tei.

Dragon Boat race at Sha Tin

The religious origins of the **Tuen Ng Dragon Boat Festival** are obscure. According to one story, during the Zhou Dynasty (1122–221BC), a loyal official, Qu Yuan, committed suicide by throwing himself into the river when his suggested reforms were rejected. Too late to save him, fishermen threw rice dumplings into the water to prevent the fish from eating his body. The incident is marked by eating glutinous rice cakes filled with meat called *zhongzi*, and boat races. The **International Dragon Boat Races** take place after Tuen Ng at Sha Tin in June or July, and often attracts teams from as many as 15 countries.

Local people burn paper offerings outside their shops and homes to placate lost souls during the **Hungry Ghost Festival** in August. This festival is not marked by a public holiday.

Mid-Autumn Festival, also known as the Moon or Lantern Festival, is held in September during the full moon. During this ancient harvest festival, delicacies called mooncakes,which are filled with sweet bean paste and salted egg, are eaten, and families gather with brightly coloured lanterns in parks and beaches to watch the moon.

CONTEMPORARY EVENTS

Modern festivals and events are essentially a manifestation of Western culture in Hong Kong. The following are worth checking out.

The **City Festival** (www.hkfringe.com.hk) in January/February offers an avant-garde programme of contemporary arts, which acts as a curtain raiser to the month-long **Hong Kong Arts Festival** (www.hk.artsfestival.org), held in February/March. This attracts more established musicians, dancers and theatrical performers from the world circuit.

The well-regarded **International Film Festival** (www.hkiff.org.hk) in March/April screens more than 100 films over a two-week period, including a few premieres, usually of Chinese films.

Since 2000, the **International Literary Festival** (www.festival.org.hk), held in April, has showcased quality English-language writing with an Asian flair, while **Le French May's Festival** of Arts (www.frenchmay.com) in May offers more eclectic fare, from music and architecture to dance and food.

Modern Architecture

The metropolis has plenty to offer in the field of contemporary high-rise architecture. Sir Norman Foster used bridge-building techniques in his **Hongkong Bank** *(see page 37)*, whilst I.M. Pei chose a series of triangular surfaces for his famous landmark, the **Bank of China Tower** *(see page 36)*, the second tallest building in Hong Kong at 1,209 ft (369m).

Enthusiasts for tall buildings will also appreciate Hong Kong's tallest (and the world's fifth tallest) structure, **Central Plaza** *(see page 44)* in Wanchai (1,227ft/374m). A more recent addition is Hong Kong's third tallest building, **The Center** (1,149ft/350m) in Sheung Wan *(see page 23)*. When completed in late 2003, **International Financial Centre Two** (1,378ft/420m) in Central *(see page 34)* will take its place as the tallest building in Hong Kong.

The **Hong Kong International Airport** at Chek Lap Kok, completed in 1998, is a stunning structure, and has been voted one of the 10 greatest architectural/engineering achievements of the 20th century.

Below: monument to steel and glass – The Center
Bottom: Hong Kong International airport

FOOD AND DRINK

Hong Kong is a gourmet's paradise, offering what is arguably the best Chinese food in the world. Excellent food from neighbouring Asian countries is also found in abundance. Western cuisine is well represented by restaurants in the more expensive hotels and in the numerous chic eateries of Lan Kwai Fong, SoHo, Causeway Bay, and Knutsford Terrace in Tsim Sha Tsui.

DIM SUM

One of Hong Kong's traditional delicacies is *yum cha* ('drink tea') or *dim sum* (literally 'touch the heart'), snacks originally served with tea at breakfast, but which today are more popular as a brunch. They are generally small savoury appetisers, such as *ha gau* (shrimp dumplings), *siu mai* (pork dumplings), *cha siu bau* (barbecued pork bun), *chun gun* (spring roll) and *dun tat* (sweet egg tart).

In traditional *dim sum* restaurants, diners pick from trolleys pushed around by waiting staff. Each plate taken is marked on a card and later tallied. But in many restaurants, menus have replaced the trolleys.

CANTONESE CUISINE

Cantonese cuisine is the most well-known Chinese food in the world as the region of Guangzhou was where many emigrants originated. Most overseas Chinese restaurants have adapted their food to appeal to local tastebuds, but generally, native Cantonese cuisine does not overpower the senses with the use of pungent sauces or spices. As in any coastal province, fresh seafood is popular, usually steamed or braised quickly and served with a simple soy-based sauce. Chicken and pork are the most popular types of meat. An innumerable variety of green leafy vegetables are eaten, usually briefly stir-fried in a wok with garlic and oil. In a typical Cantonese meal, steamed white rice is the staple, accompanied by an array of side dishes – usually a soup, a meat or seafood dish and a vegetable stir fry.

Expensive speciality dishes, using rare ingredients believed to have fortifying effects, are usually served at weddings and other festive occasions. Sharks' fin, said to be an aphrodisiac, is prepared as soup (and unnecessarily contributing to the decline of sharks worldwide); abalone is claimed to be strengthening; birds' nests, purported to ease asthmatic attacks, are actually the saliva which swallows produce to bind their nests together.

DRINKS

The perfect compliment to Chinese food is Chinese tea, which is claimed to have digestive properties. Beer is

> **Other Chinese cuisines**
> In Northern China, filled dumplings (*jiaozi*) are a popular speciality, as is Peking Duck. When cooked, the crispy skin is sliced off and served with a thin pancake, fresh scallions and *hoisin* sauce. Advance orders must be placed for Beggar's Chicken, stuffed with spices, wrapped in lotus leaves and encased in clay before baking.
>
> The southwestern province of Szechuan is famous for its spicy cuisine, redolent with garlic and chilli peppers. Chiu Chow cuisine focuses on fresh seafood; oyster omelettes are typical. Shanghainese cuisine too showcases salt- and freshwater fish, eels, prawns and crabs; sweet-and-sour fried fish originated here.

Opposite: roasted fowl is a Hong Kong speciality

another popular accompaniment and is more palatable than Chinese wine, which can be very sweet, or quite fiery. European and New World wines are quite expensive in Hong Kong restaurants, but are widely available.

Rapping one's knuckles

The custom of rapping one's knuckles on the table is based on an old story in which a Chinese emperor who liked to travel incognito throughout his realm, arrived at an inn accompanied by his official entourage. He courteously poured tea into the dishes of his subjects, who normally would have shown their gratitude by kowtowing to him. By doing so, however, they would have betrayed the emperor's identity. To avoid this, one of the courtiers suggested bending two fingers and rapping on the table in imitation of the kowtow, which would go unnoticed by onlookers.

FOOD CULTURE AND ETIQUETTE

In Asia, eating is a group activity; it would be considered rude for any individual to order a single dish for personal consumption. People enjoy going to a Chinese restaurant with a large group; this makes for livelier conversations and the chance to order a variety of dishes. The host may choose the menu, or a consensus is arrived at with a colourful parade of meat, fish and vegetable dishes, in which sweet, sour, hot, salty and bitter flavours contrast in much the same way as textures: crisp and soft, as well as wet and dry.

All serving dishes are placed in the middle of the table and the guests simply help themselves using chopsticks. At formal banquets it is considered polite for the host to select and place the choicest morsels on the guest's plate. This procedure is repeated during each course, and toasts are exchanged several times.

If tea is being drunk, the host always tops up the cups of his guests before serving himself. The guest should indicate his thanks by rapping lightly several times on the table with the knuckles of his right hand.

When the meal ends – it is polite to leave a little on the plate to indicate the abundance of the meal – the company usually breaks up fairly quickly. It is not customary to remain seated and chat once the meal is over. The bill is usually settled by a single person. It would cause considerable embarrassment in any Hong Kong restaurant, irrespective of type, if one were to request separate bills. It is better to repay an invitation in kind.

Bright lights and duck rice beckons

Restaurants

It is advisable to reserve a table in advance at the more expensive restaurants, especially on weekends and public holidays. Wait to be seated; a hostess will lead you to your table and hand you the menu, generally written in both Chinese and English.

Restaurants listed here are priced according to the following categories: $$$ = expensive; $$ = moderate; $ = inexpensive

CANTONESE

Dynasty, 3/F, Renaissance Harbour View Hotel, 1 Harbour Road, Wanchai, tel: 2584 6971 (also in Tsim Sha Tsui). Opulent Cantonese restaurant decorated in Tang-Dynasty style. $–$$
Dim Sum, 63 Sing Woo Road, Happy Valley, tel: 2834 8893. Classic *dim sum* with a laid-back yet classy ambience. The menu thoughtfully includes colour pictures of the dishes. $$
Fook Lam Moon, 35 Johnston Road, Wanchai, tel: 2866 0663 (also in Tsim Sha Tsui). A classy spot for Cantonese and *dim sum*, favoured by local celebrities. Pricey but worth it. $$$
House of Canton, 5/F, The Lee Gardens, 33 Hysan Avenue, Causeway Bay, tel: 2907 3888. *Dim sum* at lunchtime, Cantonese specialities with a few Northern dishes at night. $$
Jade Garden, Star House, 4/F, Tsim Sha Tsui, tel: 2730 6888 (and other locations). Excellent *dim sum* till 5pm – order from the English menu. Beautiful harbour views. $–$$
Luk Yu Tea House, 24–26 Stanley Street, Central, tel: 2523 5463. 1930s-style tea house famous for its delicious *dim sum*, dark wooden booths, brass spittoons and surly service. $$–$$$
Steam and Stew Inn, 21 Tai Wong Street East, Wanchai, tel: 2529 3913. Authentic MSG-free Cantonese and Shanghainese cuisine in a relaxed,

Choices, choices!
The selection below represents only a fraction of what is available in Hong Kong. For further information, visitors should consult the latest dining out publications released by the Hong Kong Tourism Board and available from HKTB Visitor Information Centres, and reviews in *HK Magazine*, issued every Friday and free of charge at many restaurants.

homely setting; popular with local politicians. Reservations essential. $$–$$$
Yung Kee, 32–40 Wellington Street, Central, tel: 2522 1624. Traditional restaurant specialising in roast goose. Cheap, cheerful, brash and noisy. $$$

OTHER CHINESE

American Peking Restaurant, 20 Lockhart Road, Wanchai, tel: 2527 1000. A popular Chinese restaurant serving Peking Duck that's mentioned in *The World of Suzie Wong*. Good value. $$
Carrianna Chiu Chow, 2/F, Hilton Tower, 95 Granville Road, Tsim Sha Tsui East, tel: 2724 4828; (also at 151 Gloucester Road, Wanchai). Chiu Chow cuisine with good goose and chicken dishes. $$
City Chiu Chow, 1/F, East Ocean Centre, 98 Granville Road, Tsim Sha Tsui, tel: 2723 6226. Specialises in seafood; try the oyster omelettes and braised squid rolls. $$
Kublai's, 3/F, One Capital Place, 18 Luard Road, Wanchai, tel: 2529 9117. Fill your dishes at the buffet and have them cooked Mongolian style on hot plates in the kitchen. Excellent value. $
Lao Ching Hing, Novotel Century Hong Kong Hotel, 238 Jaffe Road, Wanchai, tel: 2598 6080. One of Hong Kong's top Shanghainese restaurants known for its *xiao long bao* (dumplings) and crab dishes. $$–$$$

Service charge
Most restaurants automatically add 10 percent service charge to the bill. However, the waiting staff do not normally receive this money. If service is good, leave an additional tip for them.

New Silk Road, 1/F, Low Block, Grand Millennium Plaza, 181 Queen's Road, Central. Excellent Uygur food, song and dance, from northwestern China. Don't eat too much or you won't be able to join in the dancing afterwards. Try the fiery 'big-plate chicken' and traditional lamb kebabs. *Halal*, ie appropriate for Muslims. **$$$**

Peking Garden, Basement, Alexandra House, Central, tel: 2526 6465 (and several other locations). Enjoyable introduction to northern Chinese cuisine, with daily noodle-making performances. **$$**

Peking Shui Jiao Wang (Beijing Dumpling King), 118 Jaffe Road, Wanchai, tel: 2527 0289. No frills here, but great Beijing dumplings (vegetarian also available) and braised string beans. Great value. Note that the sign outside is only in Chinese, so look for the street address (English menu available). **$**

Shanghai Garden, Hutchison House, 10 Harcourt Road, Central, tel: 2524 8181. Shanghai cuisine with several good eel dishes, prawns and soya bean curd specialities. **$$**

Spring Deer, 38 Mody Road, Tsim Sha Tsui, tel: 2723 3673. A local institution for Peking Duck and other Northern specialities. Around the corner from Nathan Road. **$$**

OTHER ASIAN

Gaylord, 1/F, Ashley Centre, 23-25 Ashley Road, Tsim Sha Tsui, tel: 2376 1001. North and South Indian cuisine with seafood and vegetarian dishes. **$$$**

Indochine 1929, California Tower, 30–32 D'Aguilar Street, Central, tel: 2869 7399. An extravagant but classy Vietnamese place with a French-colonial feel; in Lan Kwai Fong. **$$$**

Kath+Man+Du, 11 Old Bailey Street, Central, tel: 2869 1298. Mouthwatering Nepalese cuisine with a cosy atmosphere. **$$**

Korea Restaurant, 58 Leighton Road, Causeway Bay, tel: 2577 9893. A long-standing, authentic Korean restaurant. Korean BBQ and more; great set lunches. **$–$$**

Kyoto Joe, G/F, The Plaza, 21 D'Aguilar Street, Central, tel: 2804 6800. Avant-garde Japanese sushi and sashimi; sister restaurant Tokio Joe is just up the street in Lan Kwai Fong. Expensive, but very chic. **$$$**

Mughal Room, 175–77 Wyndham Street, Central, tel: 2524 0107. Excellent Indian restaurant; not cheap, but outstanding Tandoori dishes. **$$$**

Perfume River, 89 Percival Street, Causeway Bay, tel: 2576 2240. Vietnamese cuisine in a simple, café-style restaurant. Good value. **$**

Phukets, 30 Robinson Road, Central, tel: 2868 9672. A long-standing Thai favourite in the Mid-Levels area. **$$–$$$**

MIDDLE EASTERN

Habibi, 112–114 Wellington Street, Central, tel: 2544 9298. Welcome to a Cairo-esque bazaar from the 1930s, with high ceilings, dazzling mirrors, hubble-bubble pipes and even belly dancers. Authentic, delicious Egyptian food. Book in advance. Available for deli-style take-out at adjacent Koshary Café. *Halal* **$$–$$$**

Zahra, 409A Jaffe Road, Wanchai, tel: 2838 4597. A fabulous tiny Lebanese restaurant with never-fail food. Reservations are a must. Dinner only, Monday to Saturday. Closed Sunday. **$$–$$$**

WESTERN

Amaroni's Little Italy, 231 Queen's Road East, Wanchai, tel: 2891 8855 (also in Kowloon Tong). Authentic Italian favourites in a casual setting. Huge portions; ideal for large groups. $–$$

The Annexx, 4/F, California Entertainment Building, 34–36 D'Aguilar Street, Central, tel: 2877 9779. Fresh and modern cuisine from the Hudson Valley, New York. Tucked above Lan Kwai Fong with a garden-feel and open windows. Pricey but worth it. $$$

Baci, 1 Lan Kwai Fong, Central, tel: 2801 5885. The best home-made pumpkin ravioli in town. Great pizzas. $$

El Pomposo, 4 Tun Wo Lane, Central, tel: 2869 7679. Excellent but pricey Spanish tapas and seafood paella. Under the escalator; phone for directions. $$$

LA Café, 16 Harcourt Road, Admiralty, tel: 2528 2923. Burger, ribs and other standard American fare. $–$$

M at the Fringe, 2 Lower Albert Road, Central, tel: 2877 4000. Extravagant prices for wonderfully elaborate Continental cuisine; some say it's the best in town. $$$

Milano, 2/F, Sun Hung Kai Centre, 30 Harbour Road, Wanchai, tel: 2598 1222. Quality Italian cuisine in an *al fresco* setting – one of very few downtown – overlooking Victoria Harbour. $$

The Mistral, Grand Stanford Inter-Continental Hotel, 70 Mody Road, Tsim Sha Tsui East, tel: 2731 2870. Where real Italians go for mama's home cooking. Hearty food, warm ambience. $$$

Morton's of Chicago, 3/F, Entertainment Building, 30 Queen's Road Central (also in Tsim Sha Tsui). Probably the best steaks in Hong Kong, priced accordingly. Fabulous soufflés as well. $$$

SoHo SoHo, 9 Old Bailey Street, Central, tel: 2147 2618. Modern British cuisine: meaning good Continental eats. Yummy sticky toffee pudding. $$$

Vong Restaurant and Bar, 25/F Mandarin Oriental, tel: 2825 4028. Stylish eaterie with a menu inspired by French and Asian cuisines. Wonderful views of Victoria Harbour. $$$

Getting a bite and a break

NIGHTLIFE

Well known for its vibrant and varied nightlife, Hong Kong offers a wide choice of nightclubs, from local bars, to Western-style watering holes and plush cabaret restaurants.

Karaoke is popular with the locals. It's possible to book a private room for your crooning friends. **California Red Box** and **Green Box** have several locations but the staff don't speak much English; try **V-Mix** (8 Sugar Street, tel: 2137 9888) in Causeway Bay.

The younger set mostly heads for the bars and clubs on and off Lan Kwai Fong and SoHo (South of Hollywood Road) above the Central District. Tsim Sha Tsui also offers a selection of bars and pubs, many of them on Ashley Road or the side streets off Carnarvon Road. At present, Hong Kong's top nightclubs are **JJ's** at the Grand Hyatt and **Club ing** in the Renaissance Harbour View Hotel.

Areas to avoid for their sleazy reputation and dubious dressed-up brothels are Wanchai and Tsim Sha Tsui East. Unfortunately, these parts of Hong Kong have still to shake off their 'Suzie Wong' image and they have a plethora of extraordinarily expensive so-called 'hostess bars', catering to a predominantly business clientele. All of which are best avoided.

> **Food first**
> Before setting out to paint the town red, make sure your tanks are well filled. To dine with a spectacular view of the harbour, try the Verandah at Repulse Bay or eateries along Stanley Main Street. Alternatively, take a ferry to Lamma or Cheung Chau for harbour-side seafood restaurants. On clear nights, Café Deco and the Peak Café at Victoria Peak feature breathtaking views. Book in advance.

BARS/CLUBS/PUBS

Agave, 27–29 D'Aguilar Street, Lan Kwai Fong, tel: 2521 2010. Fabulous, margaritas; over 100 varieties of tequila. Possibly the best Mexican food in town.

Alibi, 73 Wyndham Street, Central, tel: 2167 1676. A very 'in' place to be seen late nights. Bar and café downstairs, cosy contemporary French dining upstairs.

Al's Diner, 27–39 D'Aguilar Street, Lan Kwai Fong, tel: 2869 1869. A pioneer of the LKF area. Try their famous jello shots.

Bahama Mama's, 4–5 Knutsford Terrace, Tsim Sha Tsui, tel: 2368 2121. A Caribbean-inspired bar with reggae, funk and a dance floor.

Big Apple Pub and Disco, 20 Luard Road, Wanchai, tel: 2529 3461. An after-hours dance venue-cum-raunchy singles' nightspot.

Carnegie's, 53–55 Lockhart Road, Wanchai, tel: 2866 6289. Good, old-fashioned fun, American style. Where else can you dance on the bar top?

Club Feather Boa, 38 Staunton Street, Central, tel: 2857 7156. Stella's antique-shop-turned-bar; looks like your grandmother's living room and every bit as cosy.

Cubana, 47B Elgin Street, Central, tel: 2869 1218. Live Cuban music Sunday and Monday, good tapas and *mojitos*.

Drop, Basement, 39–43 Hollywood Road, Central, tel: 2543 8856. Low tables, high ceilings, cool sounds and always a queue at the door.

Club ing, 4/F, Renaissance Harbour View Hotel, 1 Harbour Road, Wanchai, tel: 2836 3690. Packed with executives and hot young things shaking their bootie to live bands and deejay.

East End Brewery, Sunning Plaza, 10 Hysan Avenue, Causeway Bay, tel:

2577 9119. Casual patio-style bar with good selection of beers.

In-V, 17–19/F, New World Renaissance Hotel, 22 Salisbury Road, Tsim Sha Tsui, tel: 2734 6640. Happening place, with live music and a deejay, plus karaoke rooms, cigar and fine wine bar and lots of dancing.

JJ's, Grand Hyatt Hotel, 1 Harbour Road, Wanchai, tel: 2588 1234. Hong Kong's premier, most enduring nightclub, with live music and a disco floor. Favoured by local and visiting glitterati. Dress code.

Dusk till Dawn, 78–84 Jaffe Road, Wanchai, tel: 2528 4689. A lively, often-packed, fun bar with an excellent live Filipino cover band.

Red Rock, 57–59 Wyndham Street, Central, tel: 2868 3884. Trendy Continental restaurant and bar with an excellent international beer selection and an outside terrace. Late-night dancing.

LIVE MUSIC

27 Restaurant and Bar, 27/F, Park Lane Hotel, 310 Gloucester Road, Causeway Bay, tel: 2839 3327. Live lounge music every Tuesday to Saturday from 9.30pm.

Blue Door, 5/F, 37 Cochrane Street, Central, tel: 2850 7076. A new jazz club with live music every Friday and Saturday from 10.30pm; no cover charge.

The Edge, Shop 2, G/F, The Centrium, 60 Wyndham Street, Central. A new live music venue (nightly from 10pm) with a specially designed sound system. Regular house band, guest bands and a Latin night once weekly.

The Music Room, 2/F, 34–36 D'Aguilar Street, Lan Kwai Fong, tel: 2845 8477. Formerly the Jazz Club; now a venue for a whole range of international and local live acts.

Ned Kelly's Last Stand, 11A Ashley Road, Tsim Sha Tsui, tel: 2376 0562. Live music nightly (except Sunday) from 9.30pm at this rip-roaring, good-time Australian pub.

> ### Gay scene
> There is a small but thriving gay scene in Hong Kong. In Central, **HOME** (2/F, 23 Hollywood Road, tel: 2545 0023) features an after-midnight happy hour and throbs with gay and straight folk dancing till the wee hours. **Tower Club** (20-22 D'Aguilar Street, tel: 2525 6118) is where Lan Kwai Fong's gay boys hang out. For dancing, head to *the* gay bar **Propaganda** (1 Hollywood Road, tel: 2868 1316), with metallic glitter and glitz plus plenty of dark corners.

A bustling bar at Lan Kwai Fong

SHOPPING

Hong Kong continues to be a shopping paradise, but it has long ceased to be a bargain, particularly for electronics – inflation and exorbitant rents have pared down the difference between local and European prices. Be wary of tricksters who sell fake goods in original packages, and be sure to obtain an international guarantee.

Recommended are member outlets of the HKTB's Quality Tourism Services scheme, recognisable by a sign on the door of a small red junk on a white background beneath a stylised Chinese character. The QTS website (www.qtshk.com) lists QTS-accredited shops and restaurants.

Should you encounter problems, register a complaint with the Hong Kong Tourism Board's hotline (tel: 2508 1234), but don't expect miracles. Or contact the **Consumer Council** (tel: 2929 6111).

Note that cultural differences and nuances of Cantonese may make some shopkeepers appear rude and impatient. Don't take it personally.

TAILORS
Hong Kong tailors are renowned for their skills; those who have suits made here may never wear off-the-peg again. Be wary of so-called 24-hour tailors, as such 'bargains' are rarely what they seem. A good bespoke shirt runs about HK$250, a suit around HK$2,300.

Tailor Kwan (Creative) and **Yuen's Tailors** (in the Central Escalator Link Alley of the Central Market) are recommended on Hong Kong Island. In Tsim Sha Tsui, try **Nita Fashions** (16 Mody Road), **William Cheng & Son** (8/F, 38 Hankow Road) or **Sam's Tailor** (Burlington Arcade K, 92–94 Nathan Road).

MALLS
Shopping centres are a great air-conditioned alternative to bustling street markets during the sweltering summer, and feature top brand names plus glitz and glamour.

Best bets on Hong Kong Island are the exclusive **Landmark** and **Prince's Building** in Central, **Pacific Place** in Admiralty, **Times Square** in Causeway Bay and **Cityplaza** in Taikoo Shing. In Kowloon, there are the **New World Centre** and **Harbour City** complex in Tsim Sha Tsui, and **Festival Walk** in Kowloon Tong.

> **Factory outlets**
> As an exporter of brand-name clothing, Hong Kong is invariably left with plenty of samples and overruns, which it sells at a discount. Such 'factory outlets' are concentrated near the intersection of Johnston and Luard roads in Wanchai, along Lee Garden Road in Causeway Bay and on Fa Yuen Street near the Prince Edward MTR station (exit B2).

MARKETS
Be sure to visit at least one of the lively street markets during your stay. **Cat Street** (Upper Lascar Row) off Hollywood Road in Sheung Wan offers everything from antique and reproduction works of art to Chairman Mao memorabilia. In Central, **Li Yuen Streets East & West** ('The Lanes') hawk inexpensive clothes, handbags, costume jewellery and household goods in a true bazaar atmosphere. Anyone planning a costume party should head for **Pottinger Street** for haberdashery, brightly-coloured wigs, tiaras, feather boas and masks.

Off **Queen's Road East** in Wanchai, it's easy to get lost in the labyrinthine daytime markets, full of seasonal fresh fruit and pressed ducks. In Causeway Bay, browse at **Jardine's Crescent** (till 10pm) for garments, accessories and household goods, and **Jardine's Bazaar** for dried foods. One of the best buys from the dried food-stuff stores is cashew nuts.

On the south side of Hong Kong, **Stanley Market** features brand-name clothing, Chinese paintings, backpacks and sport shoes. Despite slightly higher prices, the coastal bus ride and idyllic seaside setting compensate.

Across the harbour in Kowloon, the Mong Kok **Ladies' Market** (noon–10.30pm) on Tung Choi Street sells plenty that is fun to have – beaded handbags, stuffed cartoon character toys, lingerie and silk blouses. Then check out the **Jade Market** (10am–3.30pm) on Kansu Street, Yau Ma Tei, or the **Flower Market** (10am–6pm) off Prince Edward Road West. Cap the day with a visit to the **Temple Street Night Market** for shirts, gadgets and cheap CDs.

ASIAN ARTS, ANTIQUES, HANDICRAFTS AND FURNITURE

A thriving centre for Asian arts and crafts, Hong Kong offers plenty of near museum-quality antique furniture, carpets, sculpture, ceramics and

> **Haggle before paying**
> Although department stores and retail shops have fixed prices, bargaining is an almost essential part of the game elsewhere. Cash usually ensures a better deal, but don't expect a huge discount.

traditional paintings. Easier on the pocketbook are reproduction 'antique' Chinese furniture and Asian woodwork and handicrafts.

Find antiques in the high-rent shops along **Hollywood Road** and **Upper Wyndham Street** in Central, and malls like **Pacific Place** and **New World Centre**. **Teresa Coleman Fine Arts** (79 Wyndham Street) offers an exquisite choice of textiles, paintings and Tibetan chests.

Chinese department stores are a great place to pick up contemporary arts and crafts, from teapots and calligraphy sets to traditional silk clothing – or more practical items, like a new suitcase to carry everything. **Chinese Arts and Crafts (HK) Ltd** operates branches in Pacific Place, Wanchai's China Resources Building and Star House, Tsim Sha Tsui. Slightly less expensive is **CRC Depart-**

Hollywood Road antique shop

ment Store Ltd (Queen's Road Central, Causeway Bay and Mongkok). **Yue Hwa Chinese Products** (at 143–161 Nathan Road, Tsim Sha Tsui, and 301–309 Nathan Road, next to the Jordan MTR station) is also a good bet.

For reproduction Chinese rosewood furniture, **Queen's Road East** is the place. Competitively priced Chinese, and Southeast Asian furnishings, antiques and housewares, can be found in Aberdeen's wholesale warehouses: **Horizon Plaza** (2 Lee Wing Street) and **Hing Wai Centre** (7 Tin Wan Praya Road, Ap Lei Chau). Bus No 671 in front of Mitsukoshi (Causeway Bay) runs directly to Horizon Plaza.

> **Bait and switch**
> When shopping for electronic products, beware the 'bait and switch' tactics, wherein customers decide on a certain model, then shopkeepers surreptitiously wrap and present a cheaper model. Keep receipts, resist pressure tactics and call in the local police (tel: 999) if you are being hassled.

ELECTRONICS

Hong Kong rarely has the cut-rate prices on electronics that it used to, although the latest technologies are available. Electronic shops selling video cameras and DVD/MP3/CD players cluster in **Causeway Bay** and **Tsim Sha Tsui**. For fixed-price stores, retail chains **Broadway Photo Supply** and **Fortress** are good options.

Nathan Road contains a number of camera shops, though most local professional photographers shop along Stanley Street (**Photo Scientific Appliances**) and do their photo developing on Stanley and Wellington streets (**Colour Six, Robert Lam, East Asia Photofinishing**).

Seek out laptops and handheld PDAs at the **Windsor House** Computer Mall in Causeway Bay, **Wanchai Computer Centre** and **Star Computer City** in Tsim Sha Tsui's Star House.

FOOD, TOILETRIES & MEDICINE

For basic Western and Chinese food, supermarkets **Park 'N Shop** and **Wellome** are everywhere. Top-of-the-line imported foods are sold at **Oliver's Delicatessen** (Prince's Building; Ocean Terminal), **City Super** (Times Square; Harbour City) and **Great** (Seibu, Pacific Place).

Watson's and **Mannings** are the largest chains specialising in toiletries and drugs. For perfumes and cosmetics, try **Fanda Perfume** or **SaSa**.

Cameras are a good buy

PRACTICAL INFORMATION

Getting There

BY AIR

Hong Kong is served by dozens of airlines, including its flagship carrier Cathay Pacific (www.cathaypacific.com). All now land at the world's biggest airport terminal, the Hong Kong International Airport, opened in July 1998 in Chek Lap Kok, on the north shore of Lantau Island. While there may be some who miss the heart-stopping final approach through high-rises to the old Kai Tak airport, Chek Lap Kok's light and airy glass structure with its aerodynamically curving roof, set against the backdrop of Lantau's mountains, has won many fans.

The fastest way to and from Chek Lap Kok is by the high-speed **Airport Express Line (AEL)** railway, which links the airport to Hong Kong Station in Central in 23 minutes, with stops at Tsing Yi, and Kowloon Station near Tsim Sha Tsui. Tickets to/from Hong Kong Station cost HK$100 for one-way or same-day return, and HK$180 roundtrip (valid one month); to/from Kowloon Station HK$90 and HK$160, respectively. Trains depart every 10 minutes, 6am–1am.

Airport Express passengers can take free shuttles between the Hong Kong and Kowloon stations to more than 30 hotels, the Hung Hom KCR station and the China Ferry Terminal. MTR underground railway connections at Tsing Yi and Hong Kong Station provide additional access.

There are also several **Airbus** and conventional franchised bus routes to choose from. Average journey time is one hour, with tickets under HK$45.

Taxis are readily available in either direction but comparatively expensive – roughly HK$250–400, including bridge and tunnel fees.

> 👁 **City check-in**
> Most airlines allow Airport Express Line passengers to check in baggage at either Hong Kong or Kowloon Station, from one day in advance to 90 minutes before departure. At press time, however, all United States-bound flights required airport check-in following the events of 9/11. Call the airline directly for the latest check-in information.

BY SEA

Hong Kong is one of the cruising hubs of Asia. Over 60 international cruise ships berth beside Tsim Sha Tsui's Ocean Terminal wharf each year. At the top end of the line, it is a port of call on round the world and exotic East tours for such famous cruise ships as Cunard's *Queen Elizabeth II* (QE2) and Royal Viking Sun, Holland America Westours' *Nieuw Amsterdam* and Radisson Seven Seas' *Song of Flower*.

Getting Around

Hong Kong has a remarkable range of public transport facilities which are both efficient and inexpensive. Some can even claim to be among the city's most famous sights.

MASS TRANSIT RAILWAY (MTR)

The underground Mass Transit Railway network (tel: 2881 8888; www.mtr.com.hk; daily 6am–1pm) runs along five inter-connecting lines serving the north side of Hong Kong Island (Island Line), Kowloon and the southern New Territories (Tsuen Wan and Kwun Tong lines), the eastern New Territories (Tseung Kwan O Line) and Lantau Island (Tung Chung Line), connecting with the Airport Express Line at Hong Kong Station and Tsing

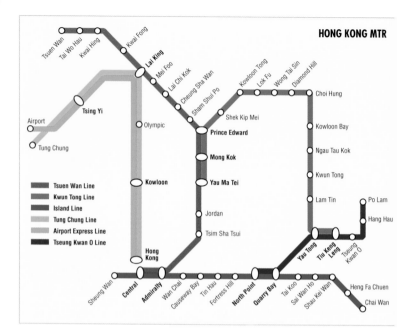

HONG KONG MTR

- Tsuen Wan Line
- Kwun Tong Line
- Island Line
- Tung Chung Line
- Airport Express Line
- Tseung Kwan O Line

Yi; and with the KCR at Kowloon Tong. Individual tickets, valid for the day of issue, range from HK$4 to HK$26. Purchase your tickets before passing through the turnstiles; the automatic ticket machines accept bills and coins. Adult fares range from HK$4 to HK$26. Octopus cards allow travel at a slight discount.

> **Octopus cards**
> Visitors staying more than a few days might find it worthwhile to buy an Octopus stored-value card (www.octopus-cards.com), which allows travel on the Airport Express, MTR, KCR, LRT and most trams, buses and ferries. The cards are available at Airport Express and MTR stations. The minimum purchase price is HK$150 which includes a HK$50 refundable deposit. Octopus cards are so popular that you can even use them to pay for purchases at convenience stores like 7-Eleven.

KOWLOON–CANTON RAILWAY (KCR)

This overland railway runs between Hung Hom in Kowloon and the Chinese border station at Lo Wu. Intermediate stations provide convenient access to towns in the New Territories; the farthest you can go without a China visa is Sheung Shui. To travel onwards to China, ticket purchases and reservations can be made at branches of the China Travel Service. Unless you are travelling on into China, the maximum fare is HK$33. It costs slightly less with an Octopus stored-value card (*see box left*). Tel: 2468 7799.

LIGHT RAIL TRANSIT (LRT)

This high-speed overland railway runs between Tuen Mun ferry pier and Yuen Long in the western New Territories. Trains operate 5.30am–12.40am daily; fares start at HK$4. Tel: 2468 7788.

TRAM

Double-decker trams rattle across the north coast of Hong Kong Island, ideal for rambles through Wanchai and Causeway Bay. The entrance is at the rear. Give yourself ample time to reach the exit at the front, where you drop HK$2 (HK$1 for under 12s) into the fare box next to the driver as you leave (or use an Octopus card). Sit on the top deck and watch the crowds. Not the quickest way to get around, though.

PEAK TRAM

For more than a century the Peak Tram (really a funicular railway) has provided the quickest way of ascending The Peak: climbing the 0.9-mile (1.4-km) route to 1,174ft (367m) in 8 minutes. The tram runs every 10 minutes until midnight. Adults HK$20 (single), HK$30 (return); under 12s HK$6 (single), HK$9 return. There is a free open-top shuttle bus from the Star Ferry concourse in Central to the lower terminus on Garden Road.

Golden oldies
Senior citizens (age 65 and up) may avail of special rates, usually half-price, on the MTR, buses and the Peak Tram. In addition, rides on the Star Ferry are free of charge for anyone over the age of 65. Fares can be paid in cash, or with special senior citizens' Octopus cards. Museum admission, too, is free or half-price for seniors.

BUSES

Double-decker buses, which run 6am–midnight, cover most of the territory. Fares range from HK$1.20 for short journeys to HK$45 for longer treks into the New Territories. Some run all night on a much-reduced frequency. Drop the fare into a box as you enter; exact fare only. Most buses now accept Octopus stored-value cards.

MINIBUSES AND MAXICABS

Minibuses and maxicabs are 16-passenger, air-conditioned, yellow vans that cover fixed routes, but usually stop anywhere to pick up passengers. To disembark, one simply shouts. Fares range from HK$2 to HK$20. However, drivers rarely speak English, which tends to make this a poor option for many tourists.

FERRIES

No visit to Hong Kong is complete without a trip across the harbour on the Star Ferry. In operation since 1898, it links the tip of Tsim Sha Tsui with Central District and covers a second route to Wanchai. At HK$2.20 (upper deck) and HK$1.70 (lower deck), it must be one of the cheapest and most scenic ferry rides in the world. Fares are paid at the automatic turnstiles at the entrance. The service runs from 6.30am–11.30pm and the crossing takes 8 minutes.

Passenger ferries also run to the islands of Cheung Chau, Lamma, Lantau and Peng Chau from the Central Ferry Piers in front of Hong Kong Station. Fares range from HK$10 on weekdays to HK$30 for a Sunday/holiday crossing on a fast ferry.

TAXI

Hong Kong's taxis have signs on the roof and a red plate proclaiming 'For Hire' on the windscreen. Red taxis patrol Hong Kong and Kowloon, green in the New Territories and blue on Lantau Island. There are extra charges for tunnel tolls, booked calls, luggage stored in the boot and luggage handling. Receipts are available on request. Flagfall is HK$12 to HK$15.

HELICOPTER

Heliservices (www.heliservices.com.hk; tel: 2802-0200) operates aerial flightseeing tours of Hong Kong, at HK$5,000 for 30 minutes and HK$10,000 for one hour. You can also charter an entire chopper from HeliHongKong (tel: 2108 9898; www.helihongkong.com) for up to 12 passengers at HK$14,250 for 30 minutes, or take the regularly scheduled flight to Macau (from HK$1,268 one way).

SIGHTSEEING TOURS

The Hong Kong Tourism Board (HKTB) arranges special tours and programmes on a regular basis, including the popular Heritage Tour, 'The Land Between' Tour, Come Horseracing Tour and Outlying Islands Escapade. Brochures are available at HKTB Visitor Information Centres.

Hong Kong Dolphinwatch (tel: 2982 1414) offers regular boat trips through the western harbour to the swimming grounds of the endangered Chinese white dolphin (*Sousa chinensis*).

Facts for the Visitor

VISAS

Most visitors only need a valid passport to enter Hong Kong. The length of a visa-free tourist visit allowed varies according to nationality. British subjects holding full UK passports are granted six months upon entry. All other European Union nationals get three months, as do nationals of Australia and the US.

CUSTOMS

Hong Kong remains a free port, and taxes are levied only on alcohol, tobacco and perfume. The tax-free allowances are one litre wine or spirits, 200 cigarettes or 250g tobacco, and 60ml perfume. If you carry firearms, they must be declared and handed over for safe-keeping until you depart. There are also stringent restrictions on the import and export of ivory, shahtoosh and other items from endan-

Useful websites
Asia Hotels (online hotel booking)
www.asia-hotels.com
Hong Kong SAR Government Information Centre www.info.gov.hk/eindex.htm
Hong Kong Tourism Board
www.DiscoverHongKong.com
Hong Kong Trade Development Council
www.tdctrade.com
Quality Tourism Services www.qtshk.com

gered species protected by CITES (Convention on International Trade in Endangered Species of Wild Fauna and Flora).

TOURIST INFORMATION

The Hong Kong Tourism Board (HKTB) is the official body representing the tourism industry in Hong Kong. Its overseas offices include:

In the UK: 6 Grafton Street, London W1S 4EQ, tel: 44 20-7533 7100.

In the US: 115 East 54th Street, 2nd Floor, New York, NY 10022, tel: 1 212-421 3382; Suite 2050, 10940 Wilshire Boulevard, Los Angeles, CA 90024, tel: 1 310-208 4582.

In Hong Kong: HKTB (www.Discover HongKong.com) operates a multilingual Visitor Hotline, tel: 2508 1234, and two Visitor Information Centres at the Star Ferry Concourse, Tsim Sha Tsui (daily 8am–6pm) and The Center, 99 Queen's Road Central (daily 8am–6pm).

There is also a Visitor Information Centre within the restricted area at the Hong Kong International Airport (daily 7am–11pm).

CURRENCY AND EXCHANGE

The local currency is the Hong Kong Dollar (HK$) which is pegged to the US Dollar at US$1 to HK$7.80. Bank notes are issued by three banks (HSBC, Standard Chartered Bank and Bank of China) and have different motifs but similar colours. They are available in the following denominations: HK$ 1,000, 500, 100, 50, 20 and 10. Coins are available to the value of HK$ 10, 5, 2 and 1 as well as 50, 20 and 10 cents.

Credit cards are widely accepted, and there are large numbers of cash dispensers. American Express cardholders have access to Jetco automatic teller machines (ATMs) and can withdraw local currency and cash traveller's cheques at Express Cash ATMs. Holders of Visa and MasterCard can also obtain local currency from the Hongkong Bank (HSBC) and Hang Seng Bank ATMs, available at most MTR stations.

Banks, licensed money changers and hotels will exchange cash and encash traveller's cheques for a small service charge. Banks generally offer the best rates. Traveller's cheques can be encashed free of charge by the issuing company: American Express, 1/F, Henley Building, 5 Queen's Road Central; Thomas Cook, 1004–5 Wing On Central Building, 26 Des Voeux Road Central.

Major banks are open Monday to Friday 9am–4.30pm, and Saturday 9am–12.30pm.

Tipping

Tipping is always welcomed. Most restaurants add a 10 percent service charge to the bill. If service is particularly good, guests should leave at least a few coins to show appreciation. Where no service charge is added, tip 10 percent (or more).

Hotel porters expect to receive HK$10–20 for carrying your luggage, or even more in top hotels. The friendly attendants in the washrooms normally receive HK$2–5.

Local people seldom tip taxi drivers, but drivers would certainly be glad if you rounded the fare up to the closest dollar.

SHOP OPENING TIMES

There are no legal restrictions; the following times may be taken as a guide:
Tsim Sha Tsui, Yau Ma Tei, Mongkok: 10am–9pm
Tsim Sha Tsui East: 10am–7.30pm
Central: 10am–6pm; many shops closed on Sunday
Wanchai, Causeway Bay: 10am–9.30pm

POSTAL SERVICES

The main post offices are next to the Star Ferry in Central and at 10 Middle Road, Tsim Sha Tsui. Both are open from Monday to Saturday 8am–6pm; Sunday and some public holidays 8am–2pm.

Numerous branch post offices have shorter opening hours and are closed on Sunday, public holidays and Saturday afternoon. Hotels usually will mail letters for guests if requested.

TELEPHONE

In principle, local calls in Hong Kong are free. In practice, most public places have payphones and local calls cost HK$1. You can make standard international direct dial (IDD) calls from public card phones with a stored-value phone card (available at HKTB Visitor Information Centres, 7-Eleven stores and some bookshops).

You can also make IDD calls from sound-proof booths and send faxes at the following PCCW shops: 10 Middle Road, Tsim Sha Tsui (tel: 2724 8322; Monday to Saturday 9am–9pm); and 147 Johnston Road, Wanchai (tel: 2892 1997; open Monday to Saturday 10am–9pm, Sunday 11am–8pm). The service centres operate on a cash or stored-value phone card basis; credit cards and cheques are not accepted.

Note that many hotels charge a 'handling fee' on local and IDD calls; inquire in advance about charges. To call Hong Kong from abroad, dial the IDD code 852 followed by the eight-digit number. There are no area codes. To call overseas from Hong Kong, dial 001 followed by area and city codes plus phone number.

Mobile phone users with roaming ability can hook into Hong Kong's GSM 900 network.

TIME

Hong Kong time is GMT plus 8 hours.

VOLTAGE

The voltage is 220V/50Hz. However, three-pin plugs of various sizes and shapes are required to fit the sockets. Adaptors are available in hotels and supermarkets.

Public holidays

The most important Western, Christian, Chinese and religious festivals are all observed. Most shops remain open for at least half a day on these special days, except during Chinese New Year, when almost everything is closed. Traditional Chinese festivals are based on the lunar calendar and therefore vary from year to year. If a festival falls on a Sunday or two festivals coincide, the day preceding or following the festival is usually designated as a general holiday.

New Year's Day: 1 Jan
Lunar New Year: Jan/Feb
Good Friday/Easter Monday: Mar/Apr
Ching Ming Festival: Mar/Apr
Labour Day: 1 May
Buddha's Birthday: May
Tuen Ng (Dragon Boat) Festival: Jun
Hong Kong SAR Establishment Day: 1 Jul
Day after Mid-Autumn Festival: Sep
China National Day: 1 Oct
Chung Yeung Festival: 14 Oct
Christmas Day: 25 Dec
Day after Christmas Day: 26 Dec

UNITS OF MEASUREMENT

Hong Kong is gradually going metric. However, property is still measured in square feet and beer in pints, while traditional Chinese measures such as the *catty* (1.5lbs/670 grams) are still used in fresh food markets and gold is sold by the *tael* (1.3 ounces/38 grams).

DISABLED VISITORS

Although buildings can be somewhat cramped, Hong Kong is a relatively easy place for disabled people to navigate. The Transport Department (tel: 2829 5223) publishes a *Guide to Public Transport Services for People with Disabilities*; an online version is also available at this website: www.info.gov.hk /td/eng/services/disable_index.html.

NEWSPAPERS

The two local English-language daily newspapers are the *South China Morning Post* and the *Hong Kong iMail*. The free entertainment listings magazines, *HK Magazine* (weekly) and *BC Magazine* (monthly), available in select restaurants, are also useful for what's going on around town.

PHOTOGRAPHY

Apart from military complexes there are no restrictions on photography. Nonetheless, photographers should bear in mind the rights of the individual to his or her privacy. Always negotiate a poser's fee before taking photos of the rickshaw drivers at the Star Ferry Concourse in Central or the Hakka women in the New Territories.

DRESS

Loose-fitting light clothing made of natural fibres is suitable almost all year round. Revealing attire and casual sports gear are not appreciated by the local residents. For all business encounters, exercise prudence and dress conservatively.

Get down to business
When doing business in Hong Kong, be sure to respect the local customs and beliefs. Do not expect to schedule meetings during Chinese New Year, as this is the most important holiday of the year, and one of the rare periods of the year when Hong Kong shuts down completely. Never underestimate the importance of business cards. Present one automatically on meeting someone by offering the card with both hands. For more advice, contact the Hong Kong Trade Development Council (www.tdctrade.com; tel: 2584 4333).

HEALTH PRECAUTIONS

During the past few years there have been a number of cases of Hepatitis A and food poisoning caused by insufficiently cooked fish and seafood from the heavily polluted Hong Kong coastal waters, or by green leafy vegetables from China which had been contaminated by pesticides.

If you are especially worried about food hygiene, avoid eating at roadside stalls and stick to hotels and smarter restaurants, many of which import jet-fresh ingredients from Australasia, the United States or Europe. Though not required for entry into Hong Kong, vaccinations against Hepatitis A and Hepatitis B are never a bad idea.

Tap water piped in from southern China meets World Health Organisation standards, though most visitors prefer to stick to bottled water, which is readily available.

The excessively cool temperatures in Hong Kong's air-conditioned buildings may lead to a chill when the weather is hot and humid outside. A simple jacket, pullover or shawl affords protection.

A sunhat and suntan lotion are necessary for extended periods outdoors. You'll need mosquito repellent at dusk in rural areas.

MEDICAL

Most hospitals offer services to a high medical standard. The doctors are trained in Western or Chinese medicine and usually speak English as they have studied abroad. Treatment must be paid for in cash; check with your health insurance company beforehand concerning the procedure for claiming reimbursement.

Medicines are widely available. Doctors often sell the necessary medicines in their clinics; chemist's shops (try Watson's or Manning's) are also well stocked. Travellers should always bring along adequate supplies of commonly used medicines and prescription drugs.

Hotels will be able to assist if you need a doctor in an emergency. For ambulance or other emergency service, dial 999.

DIPLOMATIC REPRESENTATION

Australia, Harbour Centre, 21-4/F, 25 Harbour Road, tel: 2827 8881.
Canada, One Exchange Square, 14/F, Connaught Place, tel: 2810 4321.
UK, 1 Supreme Court Road, Admiralty, tel: 2901 3000.
USA, 26 Garden Road, Central, Hong Kong, tel: 2523 9011.

Useful telephone numbers
Police, Fire, Ambulance (Emergency Service): 999
Police (Non-emergency Service): 2527 7177
Directory Enquiry: 1081
IDD Enquiry: 10013
International Direct Dial: Dial access code 001, followed by country code.
Time & Temperature: 18501
Weather: 187 8066
Hong Kong Tourism Board Visitor Hotline: 2508 1234
Transport Complaints Unit: 2889 9999

ACCOMMODATION

Hong Kong has many hotels of international standard, and virtually all the larger groups and chains have at least one establishment here.

The most expensive hotels cluster around the Tsim Sha Tsui waterfront on the Kowloon side; the HK Convention and Exhibition Centre in Wanchai; Pacific Place in Admiralty; and Statue Square in Central. These luxury establishments are continually voted among the best in the world in terms of service, facilities and cuisine.

Many tourists (and tour group operators) prefer the hotels on Nathan Road in Tsim Sha Tsui or in Causeway Bay, both lively areas with excellent transport, shopping and dining options. Hotels further up in Kowloon, in Yau Ma Tei and Mongkok, and those in older parts of Wanchai, tend to be smaller and cheaper.

As with everything else in Hong Kong, hotel rooms are pricey. Seek special rates from travel agents and online sites (www.asia-hotels.com), and find combined air ticket and accommodation packages. Remember that room rates, like visitor numbers, drop during the hot and humid summer.

Room rates for a standard double are categorised as follows:

$	= Under HK$500
$$	= HK$500–1,000
$$$	= HK$1,000–1,500
$$$$	= Above HK$1,500

Hotel Selection

HONG KONG ISLAND

The Charterhouse, 209–211 Wanchai Road, Wanchai, tel: 2833 5566; www.charterhouse.com. A cosy 'boutique' business hotel with a European feel, actually closer to the Causeway Bay MTR station than Wanchai. $$

Bargains
There are a handful of alternative hotels on Lantau Island, including the Silvermine Beach Hotel (Mui Wo, tel: 2984 8295; www.resort.com.hk; $$) and the beachside, three-roomed Babylon Villas near Cheung Sha Beach (tel: 2980 3185; $$). A more rural and spartan (but very cheap) alternative are the seven youth hostels run by the Hong Kong Youth Hostel Association (tel: 2788 1638; www.yha.org.hk).

Conrad International, Pacific Place, 88 Queensway, Admiralty, tel: 2521-3838; www.conrad.com.hk. One of the top picks for business hotels. In-room rubber duckies and teddy bears keep you company. A ridiculously convenient location, atop Pacific Place and Admiralty MTR station. $$$$

The Emperor (Happy Valley) Hotel, 1A Wang Tak Street, Happy Valley, tel: 2893 3693; www.emperorhotel.com.hk. Secluded boutique hotel near race course; 20-minute walk to the Causeway Bay MTR. Cosy, clean rooms with good restaurants and bars. $$

Excelsior, 281 Gloucester Road, Causeway Bay, tel: 2894 8888; www.excelsiorhongkong.com. A popular, compact hotel overlooking Victoria Harbour and Causeway Bay typhoon shelter; run by the Mandarin Oriental group. Convenient to shops, restaurants and five minutes to the MTR. $$$

Grand Hyatt, 1 Harbour Road, Wanchai, www.hongkong.hyatt.com; tel: 2588-1234. Experience truly palatial luxury at one of Hong Kong's finest and ritziest, right on the waterfront. Shares a beautiful outdoor swimming pool with the Renaissance Harbour View. Connected to the Hong Kong Convention and Exhibition Centre. $$$$

Ibis North Point, 136–142 Java Road, North Point, www.accorhotels-asia.com; tel: 2588 1111. A relatively new hotel with extremely compact but bright rooms. Convenient to North Point MTR station and the No A11 airport bus. Good value. **$**

Island Shangri-La Hong Kong, Pacific Place, 88 Queensway, Admiralty, tel: 2877 3838; www.shangri-la.com. The flagship of the Shangri-La group with elegant furnishings and pleasant service. Above Pacific Place. **$$$$**

JW Marriott, Pacific Place, 88 Queensway, Admiralty, tel: 2810 8366; www.marriotthotels.com. A well-designed hotel offering views of Victoria Harbour, the city or the Peak. Above Pacific Place and Admiralty MTR station. **$$$$**

Mandarin Oriental, 5 Connaught Road, Central, www.mandarin-oriental.com; tel: 2522 0111. Consistently rated among the best in Hong Kong; impeccable service and quality. Top food and beverage establishments include the Captain's Bar and Vong. In the heart of Central. **$$$$**

Metropark Hotel, 148 Tung Lo Wan Road, Causeway Bay, tel: 2600 1000; www.metroparkhotel.com. A fabulous new hotel (opened late 2001) in a great location: convenient to Tin Hau MTR station and buses; opposite Victoria Park. Great service, excellent value; free broadband connections in all rooms. Rooms are small but sufficient, with beautiful inlaid woodwork and stunning harbour views. **$$**

Novotel Century Harbourview, 508 Queen's Road West, Western, tel: 2974 1234; www.century-harbour-hotel.com. In the heart of the traditional Western District (near sharks' fins shops), making it convenient to the Western Tunnel (and therefore Kowloon) and close to Central. Good value. **$$**

Novotel Century Hong Kong, 238 Jaffe Road, Wanchai, tel: 2598 8888; www.century-hongkong-hotel.com. Small but adequate rooms in the heart of Wanchai, with small swimming pool, health club and Lao Ching Hing, one of Hong Kong's best Shanghainese restaurants. Near the Convention and Exhibition Centre. **$$$–$$$$**

The Park Lane, 310 Gloucester Road, Causeway Bay, tel: 2293 8888; www.parklane.com.hk. Relaxing view

---

Taxes
Except where noted as 'tax exempt', Hong Kong hotels add 13 percent tax and service charge to the final bill.

The plush JW Marriott Hotel

across Victoria Park from this attractive, well-run hotel. Prime location; relatively spacious rooms $$$

Renaissance Harbour View, 1 Harbour Road, Wanchai, tel: 2802 8888; www.renaissancehotels.com. Directly above the Convention and Exhibition Centre, with true 'harbour view' rooms overlooking the soaring HKCEC structure. Shares the Grand Hyatt's outdoor swimming pool. $$$–$$$$

Ritz-Carlton Hong Kong, 3 Connaught Road, Central, tel: 22877 6666; www.ritz-carlton.com. Elegant opulence in the heart of Central. Convenient to Central MTR station and Star Ferry; top restaurants include Toscana (northern Italian) and Lai Kar Heen (*dim sum* and Cantonese favourites). $$$$

KOWLOON

BP International House, 8 Austin Road, Jordan, tel: 2376 1111; www.bpih.com.hk. Small but comfortable rooms; north of Tsim Sha Tsui, cosily nestled in beside Kowloon Park. $$

Caritas Bianchi Lodge, 4 Cliff Road, Yau Ma Tei, tel: 2388 1111; www.caritas.org.hk/C&H/eng/main/lodge.htm. Clean, spacious rooms in well-run Catholic hostel off Nathan Road. Close to Temple Street Night Market and Yau Ma Tei MTR. $ (tax exempt)

Eaton Hotel, 380 Nathan Road, Jordan, tel: 2782 1818; www.eaton-hotel.com. Pleasant rooms and good-value restaurants. Near Temple Street Night Market, shops, and Jordan MTR. $$

Great Eagle Hotel, 8 Peking Road, Tsim Sha Tsui, tel: 2375 1133; www.gehotel.com. Conveniently located in Tsim Sha Tsui but away from the bustle; easy walk to MTR and Kowloon Park. Excellent service and nice décor; considered the 'insider's' five-star hotel by those in the know. $$$

Hotel Inter-Continental Hong Kong (formerly The Regent), 18 Salisbury Road, Tsim Sha Tsui, tel: 2721 1211; www.sixcontinents.com. An elegant hotel with fabulous harbour views from both rooms and the poolside. Luxurious, with a superb location and several fine dining restaurants. $$$$

Kowloon Hotel, 19–21 Nathan Road, Tsim Sha Tsui, tel: 2369 8698; www.peninsula.com. Small, modern business hotel tucked in behind 'The Pen'. Centrally located in Kowloon's prime commercial and entertainment district; close to MTR. $$–$$$

Kowloon Shangri-La, 64 Mody Road, Tsim Sha Tsui East, tel: 2721 2111; www.shangri-la.com. Opulent grandeur on the Kowloon side. Opposite the waterfront, with hoverferry access to Central. $$$$

Marco Polo Hong Kong Hotel, 3 Canton Road, Tsim Sha Tsui, tel: 2113 0088; www.marcopolohotels.com. One of three Marco Polo hotels along Canton Road. Elegant, Continental-styled, four-star hotel in the heart of the Harbour City complex. $$$–$$$$

Hotel Nikko, 72 Mody Road, Tsim Sha Tsui East, www.hotelnikko.com.hk; tel: 2739 1111. Luxurious Japanese business hotel with impeccable service, stunning harbour views and good Cantonese, Japanese and French restaurants. Convenient access to waterfront and ferries to Central, Kowloon KCR station, and museums. $$$

The Salisbury (YMCA), 41 Salisbury Road, Tsim Sha Tsui, tel: 2369 2211; www.ymcahk.org.hk. Well-appointed and next door to the Peninsula at a fraction of the cost. Good-value Western and Chinese set lunches available daily. $$

The Peninsula, Salisbury Road, Tsim Sha Tsui, www.peninsula.com; tel: 2366 6251. Hong Kong's oldest (1928) and most prestigious – and perhaps priciest hotel. Oozes colonial style and fabulous service. Extensively refurbished and still wonderfully elegant. Have high tea in the lobby, or a drink upstairs at Philippe Stark-designed Felix. $$$$

☀ INSIGHT COMPACT GUIDES

Great Little Guides to the following destinations:

Algarve	Goa	St Petersburg	North York Moors
Amsterdam	Gran Canaria	Salzburg	Northumbria
Athens	Greece	Shanghai	Oxford
Bahamas	Holland	Singapore	Peak District
Bali	Hong Kong	Southern Spain	Scotland
Bangkok	Ibiza	Sri Lanka	Scottish
Barbados	Iceland	Switzerland	Highlands
Barcelona	Ireland	Sydney	Shakespeare
Beijing	Israel	Tenerife	Country
Belgium	Italian Lakes	Thailand	Snowdonia
Berlin	Italian Riviera	Toronto	South Downs
Bermuda	Jamaica	Turkey	York
Brittany	Jerusalem	Turkish Coast	Yorkshire Dales
Bruges	Kenya	Tuscany	
Brussels	Laos	Venice	_USA regional_
Budapest	Lisbon	Vienna	_titles:_
Burgundy	Madeira	Vietnam	Boston
California	Madrid	West of Ireland	Cape Cod
Cambodia	Mallorca		Chicago
Chile	Malta	_UK regional_	Florida
Copenhagen	Menorca	_titles:_	Florida Keys
Costa Brava	Milan	Bath &	Hawaii – Maui
Costa del Sol	Montreal	Surroundings	Hawaii – Oahu
Costa Rica	Morocco	Belfast	Las Vegas
Crete	Moscow	Cambridge &	Los Angeles
Cuba	Munich	East Anglia	Martha's Vineyard
Cyprus	Normandy	Cornwall	& Nantucket
Czech Republic	Norway	Cotswolds	Miami
Denmark	Paris	Devon & Exmoor	New Orleans
Dominican	Poland	Edinburgh	New York
Republic	Portugal	Glasgow	San Diego
Dublin	Prague	Guernsey	San Francisco
Egypt	Provence	Jersey	Washington DC
Finland	Rhodes	Lake District	
Florence	Rio de Janeiro	London	
French Riviera	Rome	New Forest	

Insight's checklist to meet all your travel needs:

- *Insight Guides* provide the complete picture, with expert cultural background and stunning photography. Great for travel planning, for use on the spot, and as a souvenir. 180 titles.
- *Insight Pocket Guides* focus on the best choices for places to see and things to do, picked by our correspondents. They include large fold-out maps. More than 120 titles.
- *Insight Compact Guides* are fact-packed books to carry with you for easy reference when you're on the move in a destination. More than 130 titles.
- *Insight Maps* combine clear, detailed cartography with essential information and a laminated finish that makes the maps durable and easy to fold. 125 titles.
- *Insight Phrasebooks* and *Insight Travel Dictionaries* are very portable and help you find exactly the right word in French, German, Italian and Spanish.

The world's largest collection of visual travel guides and maps

INDEX